Wilburn M. (Bill) Potte
Lieutenant USN
Bombardier - Navigator
Grumman A-6E Intruder
Attack Squadron Sixty-Five
(VA-65)
June 14, 1971 — January 30, 1974
(See Front Cover and Page 49)
Carrier Air Wing 7 (CVW-7)
Assigned to:
U.S.S. Independence
(CVA-62) and (CV-62)
(1) September 16, 1971 — March 16, 1972
(2) June 21, 1973 — January 19, 1974

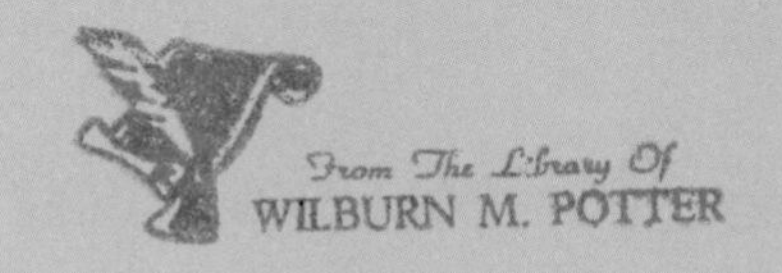

AVIATION

A-6E Intruder

Grumman's All-Weather Interdictor from Vietnam to the Persian Gulf

DAVID F. BROWN

SCHIFFER MILITARY
4880 Lower Valley Road Atglen, PA 19310

Library of Congress Control Number: 2020952762

Front cover photo courtesy of Grumman
Designed by Justin Watkinson
Type set in Impact/Minion Pro/Univers LT Std

ISBN: 978-0-7643-6276-7
Printed in China

Published by Schiffer Publishing, Ltd.
4880 Lower Valley Road
Atglen, PA 19310
Phone: (610) 593-1777; Fax: (610) 593-2002
E-mail: Info@schifferbooks.com
www.schifferbooks.com

For our complete selection of fine books on this and related subjects, please visit our website at www.schifferbooks.com. You may also write for a free catalog.

Acknowledgments

I wish to extend my gratitude to everyone who assisted me with this project: Michael Anselmo, William Barto, Jack Bol, Peter Boschert, Christina Brown, Gordon Brown, Richard Burgess, Marc Chiabaud, Jeff Cook, Jerry Cook, Molly Cooley, Mike Crutch, Michael Grove, John Hathaway, Mike Henning, Erik Hildenbrandt, Katie Hockenluber, Saburo Ioue, Jan Jacobs, Duane Kasulka, Brock Kerchner, Bert Kinzey, Joe Kistel, Ben Knowles, Samuel Lattuca, Bob Lawson, Ray Leader, Tim Lent, Jim Leslie, Don Linn, Roy Lock, Don Logan, James Lukasiewicz, Frank MacSorley, Ron McNeil, Mark Morgan, Rick Morgan, Naoki Nishimura, Lionel Paul, Ron Picciani, Troy Prince, Mick Roth, James Rotramel, Bruce Sagnor, Henk Schuitemaker, Don Spering, Sumio Suzuki, Pamela Thomas, Robert Thomas, Blaine Thompson, Bruce Trombecky, Masumi Wada, and Peter Wilson.

I am also grateful to those who assisted me in an official capacity: Alan Albrecht, USMC; Joseph Bartlett, JO2(SW), USN; Dave Buss, Cmdr., USN; Lee Corkran, SSgt., USAF; ACE Ewers, PAO, NAS Oceana; Greg Ford, Sgt., USAF; Susan Ford, PH2, USN; Jared Galloway, NNAM; Paul D. Goodrich, PH1, USN; Pamela Griffin Hansen, archivist, Northrup/Grumman History Center; Paul A. Hawthorne, PH3, USN; Jane Kinney, PH2, USN; Rory Knepp, PH2, USN; William Lipski, PH2; Marc Levitt, NNAM, USN; Mike Maus, PAO, USN; James "Gramps" McDowell, Air Operations, NAS Oceana; Donald McMichael, TSgt., USAF; Mike Menth, Cmdr., USN; R. D. Moeser, JOC, USN; Randy Morrell, PH3, USN; Steve Nakagawa, LCmdr., USN; Northrop Grumman Corporation; Attila Salman, PHAN, San Diego Air and Space Museum Archives, USN; Fred Schrupp, LCmdr., USN; Troy Snead, PAO, NAS Oceana; W. G. Taylor, Lt.(JG), USN; Vance Vasquez, PAO, USN; F. R. Volpe, PH2, USN; R. B. Williams, Sgt., USMC; and V. Zurbregg, A1C, USAF.

Dedication

In Memory of
Donald "Hawkeye" Spering

"Not sleek, never beautiful, the A-6 would soon prove itself to be a masterpiece of aeronautical engineering."
—Grumman World Publication

Contents

	Foreword	004
CHAPTER 1	G-128 to A2F-1	005
CHAPTER 2	DIANE, YA-6A, A-6A	010
CHAPTER 3	IRON HAND A-6B	012
CHAPTER 4	TRIM A-6C	017
CHAPTER 5	TEXACO KA-6D	019
CHAPTER 6	A-6E CAINS, TRAM, WCSI, SWIP, SWIP/CW	021
CHAPTER 7	Intruder II: The A-6F and A-6G	025
CHAPTER 8	Test, Training, and Operational Squadrons	026
CHAPTER 9	Combat Operations	075
CHAPTER 10	Sunset	126

Foreword

At the risk of sounding cliché, the A-6 Intruder series out of the fabled Grumman Iron Works was truly the stuff of legend. The Navy attack aircraft was noted for making its first and last deployments in combat, and this in four different decades. The type's closely knit naval aviator / naval flight officer crew performed amazing feats of aviation in multiple wars. In Vietnam, it was the Intruder, both Navy and Marine, that could get through monsoon weather that grounded practically every other strike aircraft and deliver ordnance on target. The Intruder pushed the limits of attack aircraft sensor technology and pioneered precision weapons delivery while continuing as the fleet's "Heavy Hitter" right up to its 1997 retirement.

David F. Brown, no stranger to writing about Grumman products, has done a magnificent job of covering the Intruder in its signature medium-attack role. His story is matched with superb photography, much of it his own. If you're not familiar with the A-6 and its accomplishments, you'll find them here. For those who love the Intruder, this work will probably be well received, as it highlights an aircraft that was the Navy's ultimate expression of strike warfare for many years.

Rick Morgan, LCmdr., USN (Ret.)
July 2020

A section of A-6E Intruders assigned to VA-145 over San Juan de Fuca, August 4, 1988. *Morgan*

CHAPTER 1

G-128 to A2F-1

YA2F-1 147864 was lost early in the test program after accumulating 8.6 flight hours. This view shows the thrust vectoring engine exhaust for improved STOL performance. *Grumman*

Intruder patch

Following the Korean War, the Navy determined it needed a much-improved all-weather and night attack aircraft capable of delivering conventional and nuclear weapons over great distances while hugging the terrain to avoid radar detection. Proposals for the replacement of the venerable Douglas AD Skyraider went out in the form of operational requirement CA-01504 on October 2, 1956. The Department of Defense requested a two-seat aircraft with exceptional loitering ability, capable of night and all-weather performance with short-field takeoff and landing abilities, a top speed of at least 500 knots fully loaded, and a radius of at least 300 nautical miles (nm) combat radius for close air support and 1,000 nm radius for long-range missions. Finally, this new attack aircraft had to be capable of operating from every aircraft carrier currently in fleet service. The specifications were delivered to eight manufacturers: Bell, Boeing, Douglas, Grumman, Lockheed, Martin, North American, and Vought. On January 2, 1958, Grumman's model G-128 was selected and given the USN designation A2F-1.

The YA2F-1 prototype, powered by a pair of Pratt & Whitney J52-P6 turbojets, flew for the first time on April 19, 1960, one year and four days after the first drawing was received on Grumman's shop floor. Before this achievement various approaches were followed to meet the requirements outlined, such as short takeoff and landing (STOL), two-man crew, the housing of the massive radars, and the design of the swept-back wet wing. As with previous Grumman designs, the Intruder went through a series of conceptual drawings, with G-128Q resembling the A2F-1 Intruder. The first flight, with Bob Smyth at the controls, was deemed uneventful. This initial Intruder, bureau number 147864, was followed by seven airframes numbered 147865/867 to 148615/618, all utilized in the further development of the type.

Grumman Shop #2, 147865, displaying Marine markings. This YAF-2F-1 was later remanufactured as an EA-6A and accumulated 7,390 flight hours, more than any other YA2F-1. *Grumman*

As with any new design, the need for modifications soon became apparent. To meet the STOL requirement, the prototype featured tailpipes capable of tilting down 23 degrees. Although performing flawlessly, this feature was deemed unnecessary and cost ineffective, and was thus eliminated after 148618. Another issue required the reposition of the horizontal stabilizers 16 inches rearward due to airflow fluctuations caused by the fuselage-mounted speed brakes. The fuselage speed brakes were later determined to be inadequate for their intended purposes of dive-bombing and carrier landings. The fuselage speed brakes were inactivated and replaced by wingtip brakes, known as decelerons. These proved so successful that the fuselage brakes were eliminated on later Intruders starting with 154170. One additional airframe change was ordered: enlarging the rudder's chord to improve spin recovery.

By September 18, 1962, all YA2F-1s, including 147866, were redesignated as A-6As. This example was the first to feature the repositioned horizontal stabilizer moved 16 inches aft to improve handling characteristics. Also evident is the improved rudder featuring a larger chord. T-2 on the stabilizer indicates this airframe was "tanker two," on loan to Grumman during the F-14 test program, 1973–76. *McNeil*

YA2F-1 147867 was used to test the track radar and ordnance. It flew for the first time in December 1960. Of interest is the 35 mm camera mounted to the underside just aft of the radome. *Grumman*

YA2F-1 148615 during fuel dumping tests. The number 5 and 6 Intruders were utilized to test DIANE and the search radar. *Grumman*

YA2F-1 148616 on display during Armed Forces Day 1962. Note the photo registration markings and its load of Day-Glo Mk. 82 bombs. *Via Grove*

NAS Norfolk, April 23, 1978. This forlorn NA-6A, 148617, Intruder #7, was scrapped on September 2, 1978. The T-1 denotes use by Grumman for testing aerial refueling with the F-14 Tomcat. *Spering*

Test flights uncovered complicated issues with avionics reliability, computer memory, and cooling. Additionally, there was an issue of resolution and brightness with the displays for the pilot and the bombardier/navigator (B/N). These problems and others delayed the Intruder's introduction into fleet service for more than a year. Despite these issues the Navy continued to place orders. By September 1962, sixteen Intruders had been accepted by the Navy with an additional eighty-one on order.

CHAPTER 2

DIANE, YA-6A, A-6A

The Intruder's drumstick-like design was necessary to fit two radars under its bulbous radome. The Litton AN/ASQ-61 Digital Integrated Attack Navigation Equipment (DIANE) system represented the core of the Intruder. The system consisted of the Norden AN/APQ-92, a KU-Band Search / Navigation Radar; and the AN/APQ-88 (later upgraded to AN/APQ-112) Tracking/ Attack Radar. Included with DIANE was the Litton AN/APQ-61 radar computer (with drum memory), AN/ASN-31 inertial platform, CP-729A air data computer, AN/AVA-1 vertical display, AN/APN-141 radar altimeter, AN/APN-153(V) Doppler Radar navigation set, and AN/ASQ-57 electronic control, plus TACAN, ADF, and IFF. The computer was extremely advanced, capable of delivering ordnance accurately in all weather conditions, day or night. It was capable of 100 solutions per second and calculated the exact point for weapons release regardless of dive angle, g-forces, airspeed, wind velocity, or range to the target. Once the ordnance was released DIANE would then compute the best exit from the target area.

One capability never utilized was the ability to deliver a nuclear weapon. Because it could fly fast and low under enemy radar, Intruder crews trained to use a most unusual delivery method known as the Loft Angle Bombing System–Initial Point, or LABS-IP. The approach would be made at high speed and low level. Once near the target, a steep climb to almost vertical would be initiated. The onboard computer would calculate the release point, and once the weapon was deployed, the pilot would egress the target area as quickly as possible.

The final test for any new tactical Navy aircraft is carrier qualifications. Carrier suitability trials for the Intruder were successful, and the final stage, the Board of Inspection and Survey (BIS) trials, began. The BIS trials covered all aspects of future Intruder operations. After the tests concluded the Navy officially accepted its first Intruder.

YA-6A 148618 photographed conducting touch-and-goes during suitability trials aboard USS *Enterprise*, December 1962. *Navy*

In December 1962, YA-6A 148618 recorded the second-ever nose tow catapult launch from the deck of USS *Enterprise*. Barely discernible behind the "8 Ball" is a yellow silhouette of an aircraft carrier. *USN*

A-6A 149477 was one of the first A-6As delivered to Intruder training squadron VA-42. It was photographed at NAS Oceana, Virginia, 1963. *USN*

CHAPTER 3

Iron Hand A-6B

Iron Hand missions, the Suppression of Enemy Air Defenses (SEAD), was a joint USAF and USN operation conducted during the Vietnam War from 1965 to 1973. The USAF utilized the F-100F and F-105F/G to detect and destroy Surface-to-Air Missile (SAM) sites. Initially the Navy used the A-4 Skyhawk armed with the AGM-45 Shrike for Iron Hand missions. All A-6As were wired to deliver the Shrike; the Navy required an attack aircraft dedicated to the SEAD mission possessing the capability of launching a new, more lethal antiradiation missile, the AGM-78 Standard ARM, or STARM. At 1,382 pounds the AGM-78 was a massive weapon—three times heavier than the Shrike—and the Intruder was capable of hauling four on LAU-77 weapons rails. Authorization approving the A-6B designation came down from the CNO on November 10, 1965, and the Navy decided to modify nineteen A-6As to A-6Bs.

Three variants of the A-6B emerged due to ever-changing technology and threats. These modifications were known as Mod 0, Mod 1, and PAT/ARM. The first two Mods retained the AN/APQ-92 navigation radar but required the removal of the Intruder's AN/APQ-112 tracking radar and AN/ASQ-61 ballistics computer. The primary sensor in Mod 0 was the AN/APS-107 passive sensor. Ten Intruders were so modified, and the telltale differences were small diamond-shaped antennas: two mounted on the lower part of the intakes and an additional pair mounted on either side of the upper radome. Further upgrades followed commencing in 1969, with incremental improvements from 1972. Mod 0 A-6B Intruders initially deployed with VA-75 "Sunday Punchers" aboard USS *Kitty Hawk* (CVA-63), December 1967 to June 1968.

A-6A 149957 was upgraded to A-6B Mod 0 in 1967 and reassigned to VA-75. The diamond-shaped objects on the radome and intake are AN/APS-107 homing antenna. *Via Roth*

A-6B Mod 0 cockpit. *Grumman*

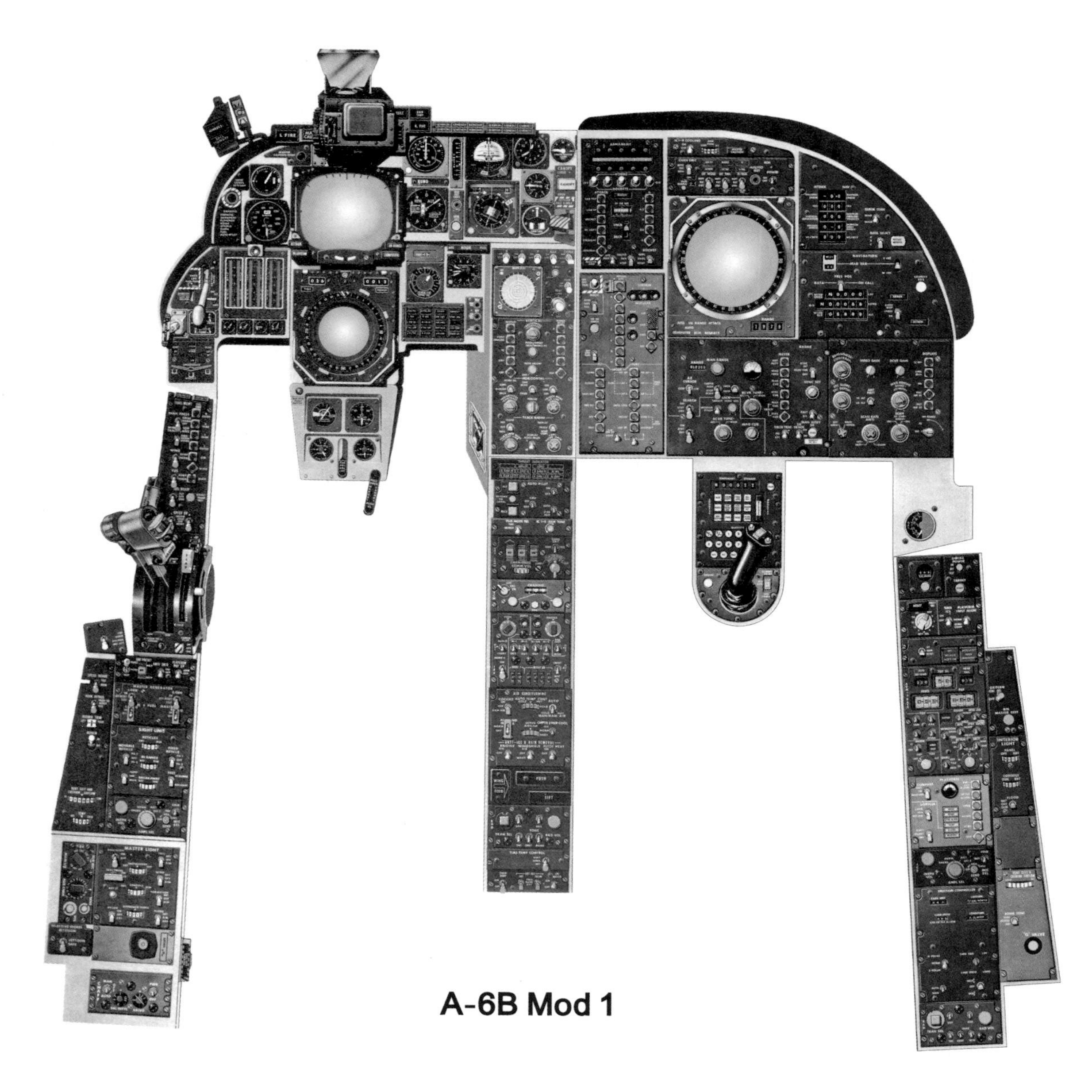

Mod 1 changes involved the installation of the AN/APS-118 Target Identification Acquisition System in five Intruders. The most notable characteristic was a series of "button" antennas on the radome—and more antennas to the base of the radome—with an additional AN/APS-118 antenna array in the tailcone. The first Mod 1, 151820, flew on October 1, 1968. As with Mod 0 A-6Bs, these Intruders also did not retain their all-weather and night attack capabilities. *USN*

The first flight of an A-6B Mod 1 took place on October 1, 1968. *Grumman*

This image shows the placement of the button antennae on the A-6B Mod 1 radome. *Convair*

The A-6B could carry four AGM-78 STARMs on LAU-77/A rails. The AGM-78A used analog control, and the AGM-78B and later models were digitally controlled. *Via Roth*

A-6B PAT/ARM (Passive Angle Tracking / Anti-Radiation Missile) involved modification of both the AN/APQ-112 radar—including the dish—the AN/APR-25, and adding the Standard ARM Mod 0/1 missile control module. These modifications enabled it to launch the AGM-78A/B/C/D. These airframes retained their all-weather/night capabilities and outwardly resembled the A-6A. This version first flew on August 26, 1968.

A-6A 155628, along with 155629 and 155630, were reconfigured as PAT/ARM Intruders. This example is loaded with a pair of inert AGM-78s. *Grumman*

CHAPTER 4

TRIM A-6C

A-6C 155667, viewed here in TRIM configuration near Long Island, New York, on April 25, 1970. *Grumman*

TRIM (Trails, Roads, Interdiction, Multi-Sensor) might be considered the father of TRAM. TRIM sensors were housed in a massive pod attached to the underside of twelve A-6A airframes modified to A-6C configuration. Following tests conducted with 147867 and one prototype, 151568, Grumman converted twelve A-6As to A-6Cs from February to June 1970. A-6C missions involved the detection and destruction of traffic along the Ho Chi Minh Trail. Upgrades included the AN/APQ-112 and the AN/APN-186 navigational radar.

Additionally, the fire control radar was improved with the installation of the AN/APQ-127, with target information displayed in video form. TRIM also alerted the crew using an audible signal and indicator light. An additional sensor, Black Crow, was used to detect engine ignitions. It was effective in all weather conditions, even when targets were concealed under a canopy of vegetation and at distances up to 10 miles. The first squadron to take the A-6C into combat were the "Boomers" of VA-165 aboard USS *America* (CVA-66), April 1970 to December 1970.

This image shows the TRIM turret in the operating position. The Low-Light-Level Television (LLLTV) windows are quartz composition glass; the Forward-Looking Infrared (FLIR) windows are of germanium composition. *Grumman*

A-6C TRIM pod in the stowed, closed position. *Author's collection*

A-6C 155688 assigned to VX-5, September 27, 1972. *Miller*

CHAPTER 5

Texaco KA-6D

In 1966, Grumman modified A-6A 149937 to demonstrate the possibility of using the Intruder as a dedicated aerial-refueling platform. *Grumman*

The Intruder as an aerial-refueling platform was successfully demonstrated to the Navy on April 23, 1966, when A-6A, BuNo 149937, refueled an F-4B. The Navy showed little interest in a dedicated tanker version of the Intruder. With the retirement of the AJ-1 Savage and the KA-3B Skywarrior being phased out of service the Navy later reversed course, authorizing Grumman to proceed with the tanker version in 1968. The first KA-6D, 151582, took to the air on April 16, 1970. Most of the DIANE equipment and associated radar was removed from KA-6D conversions.

Grumman delivered ninety KA-6Ds, converting seventy-eight older A-6As and twelve additional A-6E airframes. The conversion process involved new bulkheads, reworked outer wing panels, new front and rear beams, plus rebuilt ribs. All-new fuel cells, a complete rewiring of the airframe, and the addition of the AN/ASN-41 navigation computer coupled with a new global navigation system completed the modifications. The "Thunderbolts" of VA-176 were the first deployable squadron to receive the KA-6D on September 25, 1970.

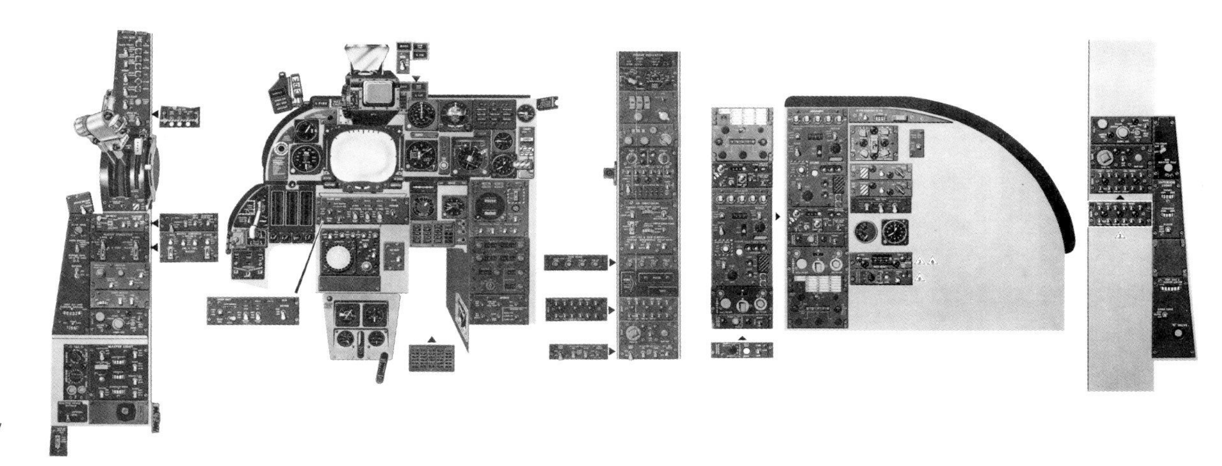

KA-6D pilot and observer positions, circa 1974. *USN*

The "Five Wet" configured KA-6D was capable of hauling 10,000 to 15,000 pounds of fuel with a transfer rate of 300 gallons per minute. *Goodrich*

As a backup, the KA-6D could carry the D-704 Buddy Store refueling pod on the centerline hardpoint. *USN*

CHAPTER 6

A-6E CAINS, TRAM, WCSI, SWIP, SWIP/CW

Grumman modified A-6A 155673 as the A-6E Prototype. This Intruder was also used as the TRAM development aircraft. *Grumman*

The prototype A-6E, 155673, flew for the first time on February 27, 1970. The first flight of a production A-6E, BuNo 158041, took place on September 26, 1971, with formal acceptance on December 1, 1971. The majority of improvements were internal, with the exception of new Electronic Counter Measures (ECM) antennas. The A-6A's outdated vacuum tube technology was replaced with a new solid-state, multimode radar in the form of the Norden AN/APQ-148. The Carrier Aircraft Inertial Navigation System (CAINS) replaced the troublesome AN/ASN-31 with the Litton Industries AN/ASN-92. The GRU-7 replaced the GRU-5 ejection seats, and the inboard wing fences were moved closer to the fuselage.

In 1974, A-6E upgrades were trialed with the addition of the Target Recognition Attack Multisensor (TRAM). The first A-6E equipped with TRAM, BuNo 155673, flew on March 22, 1974. However, the full-up production A-6E TRAM, 160995, was not ready until November 29, 1978. TRAM consisted of a gyroscopically stabilized turret mounted under the Intruder's radome. This turret housed a laser range finder/designator and IBM AN/ASQ-155 computer. These were bore-sighted colinearly with the turret's FLIR and could be slaved to the Intruder's Norden AN/APQ-156 radar, permitting the bombardier/navigator to hit targets with extreme accuracy, even moving targets via Airborne Moving Target Indicator (AMTI). TRAM sensors alone could be used without the benefit of the radar, thereby not warning the target. The Intruder was now fully capable of designating and destroying targets with laser-guided bombs without having to rely on another aircraft to "buddy-lase" the target. In addition to autonomous targeting, TRAM Intruders could use Offset Aim Point (OAP), allowing the B/N to launch a weapon at an unseen target by inputting the offset range and bearing to another nearby target. During the 1980s TRAM equipped A-6Es received a further upgrade, Weapon Control System Improvement (WCSI). As the name implies, it incorporated additional weapons such as the AGM-84 Harpoon and AGM-123 Skipper II into the Intruder's already impressive arsenal.

The TRAM/CAINS prototype A-6E 155673 on the NATC ramp, February 21, 1975. *Leader*

A-6E TRAM cockpit, 1983. *Roth*

The Systems/Weapon Improvement Program (SWIP) began in the late 1980s. This upgrade involved the addition of a co-processor to the AN/ASQ-155 so the computer could perform a digital interface via a MIL-SPEC 1553 data bus and the Intruder's pylons. Externally SWIP Intruders had an aft-facing Defensive Electronic Counter Measures antenna mounted above the fuel dump outlet. These improvements permitted the A-6E to carry and autonomously launch precision-guided weapons, including the AGM-65 Maverick, AGM-84E Standoff Land Attack Missile (SLAM), AGM-62 Walleye, and AGM-88 High-speed Anti-Radiation Missile (HARM), plus the previously discussed AGM-84 Harpoon.

A mid-1970s analysis projected the A-6 wing's life span to be 4,400 hours. The 1986 Department of Defense Appropriations hearings concluded the A-6 was designed with a wing life span of 2,200 hours. Follow up testing revealed the 2,200-hour life span was correct. As a result, a significant number of KA-6D/A-6E wings were over-age, resulting in 20% (82) of them being grounded and a further 27% (109) assigned restricted flight operations. A decision was made to rewing 85% of the surviving A-6Es. The Navy launched a competition for a new wing that was not to exceed the weight of the existing A-6E wing. Boeing won this competition with a graphite/epoxy composite design with a proposed 8,800-hour lifes pan. A total of 136 Intruders were fitted with the new "Boeing" wing.

A-6E 164384 was one of the final twenty-one new-built, SWIP-configured, composite-wing Intruders delivered. Photographed on the NAS Oceana ramp, October 20, 1995, assigned to VA-75. This Intruder is currently displayed at Grumman's Memorial Park, Calverton, New York. *Author*

CHAPTER 7

Intruder II: The A-6F and A-6G

The A-6F was conceived to bridge a gap in medium attack until the Advanced Tactical Aircraft (ATA) entered service. Known as the Intruder II, the A-6F was powered by two non-afterburning, smokeless, GE F404 turbofans providing better fuel economy and more power. The Intruder II featured the multimode Norden AN/APQ-173 synthetic aperture radar, offering better range and sharper resolution. The radar interfaced with the new AN/AYK-14 digital computer, avionics, and multifunctional displays, digital instruments, and a true heads-up display (HUD) for the pilot. Two additional wing pylons outboard of the wing fold mechanism permitted carriage of the AIM-9L Sidewinder or AIM-120 Advanced Medium-Range Air-to-Air Missile (AMRAAM). Grumman constructed five A-6Fs, 162183 to 162187. These five Intruder IIs incorporated Grumman wings, since the Boeing graphite/epoxy wing was not yet available. The program was canceled in favor of the ATA under development by McDonnell Douglas and General Dynamics as the A-12 Avenger II.

Despite the cancellation of the A-6F, Grumman proposed a less expensive version powered by J52-P408 engines and featuring the AN/APQ-173 radar and improved avionics. Grumman proposed the construction of 300 new built A-6Gs and possibly an additional 200 conversions from A-6Es. This proposal was also scuttled in favor of moving ahead with the A-12 Avenger II. On January 7, 1991, the Avenger II program also was canceled.

A-6F 162183, a propulsion and aerodynamic test bed, flew for the first time on August 26, 1987. Of interest is the distinctive bulged fuselage, a necessary enhancement to house the more powerful F-404-GE-404 engines. *Grumman*

A-6F 162185 was the third A-6F prototype. "DSD" on the vertical stabilizer stands for Digital Systems Development. This Intruder II is currently displayed at the USS *Intrepid* Museum, New York City. *Grumman*

CHAPTER 8

Test, Training, and Operational Squadrons

NATC

A-6A 149940 assigned to the Naval Air Test Center, November 22, 1975. *Author's collection*

KA-6D (K55) 149484 on the NATC ramp, June 19, 1973. The "W" indicates it was assigned to Weapons Test Directorate. *Author's collection*

A-6E TRAM 159567 loaded with colorful Mk. 7 CBUs and recording equipment for a test sortie from NATC, November 4, 1980. *Burgess*

PMTC/NMC

A-6A 151784; note the AN/AWW-7B data link pod utilized as a communications link between the aircrew and the YAGM-53A Condor mounted on the port wing. *USN*

A-6B Mod 0 151563 preparing for a test flight, Pt. Mugu, California, October 24, 1967. *USN*

Pacific Missile Test Center, A-6E 152642 with a Northrop BQM-74 Chukar drone. *USN*

NAEC LAKEHURST

A-6A 149940 photographed in March 1978 on the ramp at Naval Air Engineering Center Lakehurst, New Jersey. *Leslie*

CHINA LAKE

NA-6A 149937 assigned to Naval Weapons Center, China Lake, California, May 19, 1977. *Lock*

Delivered on October 31, 1975, A-6E 159569 spent the majority of its service life with test and training squadrons. It is pictured in November 1983, assigned to the Naval Weapons Center, China Lake. *Roth*

NAVAL AIR WARFARE CENTER

A-6E 155698 Weapons Division on May 6, 1993. The Naval Weapons Center (NWC) and the Pacific Missile Test Center (PMTC) Point Mugu were disestablished in January 1992 and joined with naval units at Albuquerque and White Sands, New Mexico, as a single command—the Naval Air Warfare Center–Weapons Division (NAWC-WD). *Vasquez*

VX-5 "VAMPIRES"

151565 was delivered on May 6, 1964, as an A-6A and upgraded four years later to A-6B Mod 0. Modified to A-6E in 1976, TRAM followed in 1983; then further improvements, including SWIP. It was in line for a new composite wing when that program was canceled. It currently rests on the floor of the Atlantic Ocean as part of the Intruder Reef. *Thompson*

A-6E 155699 assigned to VX-5, photographed at China Lake, California, February 10, 1993. *Vasquez*

NAVAL STRIKE WARFARE CENTER

Delivered on August 31, 1990, A-6E 162206 spent its short career flying with test and evaluation units. This Intruder retired to the Oregon Air and Space Museum with only 874 flight hours, ten catapult launches, and eleven arrested landings. *Grove*

VA-42 "GREEN PAWNS"/"THUNDERBOLTS"

A-6E 151573 VA-42, July 19, 1977, NAS Oceana. *Lukasiewicz*

Wearing an appealing high-viz paint scheme, KA-6D 149484 rests on the VA-42 ramp, NAS Oceana, Virginia, November 1990. *Linn*

Following the disestablishment of VA-176 on October 30, 1992, their insignia and squadron history was transferred to VA-42. A-6E 160998 was photographed on September 11, 1993, at NAS Oceana displaying the new markings. Of interest is the composite wing, identifiable by the bulged outboard pylon and white cylindrical folding mechanism. *Author*

VAH-123 "PROFESSIONALS"

A-6A 152933 assigned to VAH-123, photographed at Los Alamitos, California, July 28, 1967. With the establishment of VA-128, VAH-123 was relieved of its duties training Intruder crews. *Hathaway*

VA-128 "GOLDEN INTRUDERS"

A-6E 155621 photographed April 1, 1977, still wearing its bicentennial markings. *Henning*

Delivered as an A-6A on September 23, 1966, 152628 was converted to KA-6D (K46). It was in a "Five Wet" configuration when photographed on October 24, 1982. *Author's collection*

A-6E 154161 at NAF Washington, December 1986. The "birdcage" is in the open position, with the maintenance ladder unfolded for ease of access to the liquid oxygen bottles. *Author*

VAQ-129 "VIKINGS"

152593 was one of two A-6As assigned to VAQ-129 from 1971 to 1972 to provide flight time for instructors when the squadron had only a small number of Prowlers assigned. *Grove*

VMAT(AW)-202 "DOUBLE EAGLES"

A-6A 155651 assigned to VMAT(AW)-202, January 31, 1976. The bar-like protrusion above the fuel tank is the AN/ALQ-100 ECM antenna. *Leader*

The first new-built A-6E 158041, photographed assigned to VMAT(AW)-202, December 1985, NAF Washington. *Author*

VA-34 "BLUE BLASTERS"

151820 was one of the last A-6As to be modified to an A-6B. These last six A-6Bs were equipped with TIAS. All six were initially assigned to VA-34. *Bol*

KA-6D 149940 photographed in Intruder Country, NAS Oceana, September 10, 1987. *Author*

A-6E 152923 taxiing at NAS Fallon, Nevada, October 1995, armed with a practice CATM-88 HARM. Evidence of SWIP is the AN/ALR-67 low-band antenna array near the speed brakes. *Grove*

VA-35 "BLACK PANTHERS"

152617 was one of six A-6As converted to A-6B Mod 1 (TIAS). This example was assigned to VA-35 on June 8, 1973. *Knowles*

Black Panther KA-6D 154133 photographed on January 20, 1981. *Lawson*

A-6E 159311 VA-35, October 10, 1987, with NAS Oceana's "Intruder Country" in the background. *Author*

VA-36 "ROADRUNNERS"

A-6E 164382 VA-36 photographed April 13, 1992, preparing to launch from NAS Oceana. *Author*

A-6E 158538 VA-36 photographed at NAS Fallon, April 25, 1990, hauling an inert Paveway I Mk. 83 LGB. *Lawson*

VA-52 "KNIGHTRIDERS"

A-6A 154133 VA-52 photographed during 1968. *Picciani*

KA-6D 152626 VA-52, February 24, 1988, refueling an A-6E assigned to VA-128. *Lawson*

Delivered as an A-6A on May 2, 1968, 154161 would later be upgraded to an A-6E with TRAM, SWIP, and a composite wing. *Grove*

VA-55 "WARHORSES"

KA-6D 155597, assigned to VA-55, being repositioned aboard USS *Coral Sea* in 1986. *Knepp*

A-6E 158051 VA-55, December 12, 1988, NAS Fallon, Nevada. *Grove*

VA-65 "TIGERS"

A pair of A-6Es (158533 and 158531) assigned to VA-65, 1976. *Grumman*

KA-6D 149951, NAS Fallon, Nevada, December 1979. *Grove*

A-6E 154167, NAS Fallon, 1984. This Intruder is currently preserved at NASM's Udvar-Hazy Facility, Dulles IAP, Virginia. *Grove*

VA-75 "SUNDAY PUNCHERS"

KA-6D 152618 aboard USS *Saratoga*, January 8, 1980. *Lawson*

A-6E 157026 aboard USS *Enterprise*, April 1996. *Author*

VA-85 "BLACK FALCONS"

A-6A 151790 VA-85, 1965, returning to USS *Kitty Hawk* with three empty triple ejector racks. Due to them being the "outsider" East Coast squadron, the "Black Falcons" were assigned side numbers (modex) in the 800 range. Of interest are the rows of mission markings. *Paul*

KA-6D 152893 VA-85, NAS Oceana, April 1977, with bicentennial markings still intact. *Leslie*

A-6E 155689 VA-85, NAS Oceana, April 1994. *Author*

VA-95 "GREEN LIZARDS"

A-6A 152954 VA-95, March 1973. *Knowles*

A-6E 159312 VA-95, bicentennial markings, August 1976. *Roth*

A-6E 159895 VA-95, NAS Fallon, November 5, 1980. *Grove*

VA-115 “ARABS”/”EAGLES”

A-6A 155678 VA-115, April 1, 1975.
Author’s collection

A-6B 155629 VA-115 PAT/ARM with D-704 refueling pod. This Intruder received the following upgrades: A-6E, TRAM, SWIP, and composite wing. At one time it was displayed at the Quonset Point Air Museum.
Author’s collection

KA-6D 152911 VA-115, April 1, 1975. This Intruder was involved in the partial ejection of Lt. Keith Gallagher (the B/N) on July 9, 1991. *Wada*

A-6E 161100 VA-115, February 12, 1990. *Suzuki*

VA-145 "SWORDSMEN"

A-6A 155669, USS *Ranger*, July 1975. *Jacobs*

A-6B 151564 Mod 0/1, December 1973, NAS Fallon. *Jacobs*

KA-6D 152637 was written off on May 12, 1974, following a collision with F-4J 158357. *Jacobs*

A-6E 155595 VA-145, USS *Ranger*, October 20, 1978. This Intruder had a long, distinguished career, including combat in Vietnam and the Persian Gulf. *Lawson*

A-6E 159572 was written off on November 6, 1989, when the crew ejected following a total hydraulic failure. The Intruder impacted the water 7 miles from NAS Whidbey Island, Washington. The crew was recovered. *Author*

VA-155 "SILVER FOXES"

151576 was photographed in December 1989. The squadron received their first Intruder on November 16, 1987. The band around the fuselage aided in differentiating the KA-6D from the A-6E in flight. *Grove*

VA-155, A-6E 160429, assigned to the short-lived CVW-10, photographed aboard USS *Lexington*, November 1987. *Linn*

VA-165 "BOOMERS"

Delivered as an A-6A during January 1969, 155662 received the TRIM conversion in 1970. It was photographed in July 1970. *Inoue*

Photographed on June 2, 1981, six months after delivery to VA-165, A-6E 161107 is seen northwest of NAS Fallon, Nevada. *Lawson*

KA-6D 151821 photographed during January 1980 at NAS Whidbey Island, home to sixteen West Coast Intruder squadrons. *Burgess*

A-6E 152928 on September 11, 1989, at NAS Whidbey Island, wearing temporary camouflage for a Red Flag exercise. This Intruder was lost during Operation Desert Storm when it fell victim to ground fire while assigned to VA-155 on January 17, 1991. *Morgan*

A-6E 161686 painted as 151686 wearing a VA-196 scheme for the movie *Flight of the Intruder*. Those are not mission markings; they are camera silhouettes depicting aerial scenes shot. The name below the canopy is that of Lt. Jake "Cool Hand" Grafton, played by actor Brad Johnson. *Vasquez*

VA-176 "THUNDERBOLTS"

No Intruder scored an air-to-air kill, but A-6A 157000, assigned to VA-176, displays a MiG kill. The name on the canopy, Cmdr. Guy Cane, provides a clue. On July 29, 1968, then LCmdr. Cane used an AIM-9 to down a North Vietnamese MiG-17 while flying an F-8E assigned to VF-53. *Picciani*

A-6C, TRIM, 155688, NAS Oceana, Virginia, before VA-176's 1973 Mediterranean cruise. *Author's collection*

KA-6D 151793 VA-176, NAS Oceana, Virginia, October 1989. *Linn*

A-6E 159896, April 1991, NAS Oceana, Virginia. This Intruder is carrying a D-704 refueling pod. *Author*

VA-185 "NIGHTHAWKS"

KA-6D 154154 landing at NAF Atsugi, Japan, April 30, 1989. The squadron was forward deployed to Atsugi in September 1987. *Suzuki*

A-6E 157025 landing at NAF Atsugi, Japan, December 9, 1989. *Suzuki*

VA-196 "MAIN BATTERY"

A-6A 152626 photographed flying from USS *Constellation,* May 1967. VA-196 was the first Whidbey-based Intruder squadron deployed to the Vietnam War. *USN*

KA-6D 151810 photographed on April 27, 1985. It was written off on December 5, 1991, when it crashed into the Persian Gulf off the coast of Iraq while flying from USS *America.* The crew was recovered. *Morgan*

A-6E 154170 currently resides at the Flying Leathernecks Museum, San Diego, California. It was photographed in November 1979, serving as the Commander, Air Group, or "CAG" Bird for VA-196. *Lawson*

VA-205 "GREEN FALCONS"

KA-6D 151808, assigned to VA-205, a reserve squadron. *Grove*

VA-304 "FIREBIRDS"

KA-6D 149937, assigned to VA-304, a reserve squadron. *Grove*

A-6E 158531, assigned to VA-304. *Lawson*

VMA(AW)-121 "GREEN KNIGHTS"

A-6E 155657 VMA(AW)-121, April 1, 1977. *Grove*

A-6E 155689 VMA(AW)-121, June 1985. *Grove*

VMA(AW)-224 "BENGALS"

A-6A 152908 VMA(AW)-224, Hill AFB, Utah, May 5, 1973. *Knowles*

A-6E 155604 VMA(AW)-224. *Grumman*

VMA(AW)-224 KA-6D 151809. Only two Marine Intruder squadrons operated KA-6Ds. NL515 flew with the "Bengals" during their 1972 combat deployment to Vietnam aboard USS *Coral Sea*. *Grove*

VMA(AW)-225 "VAGABONDS"/"VIKINGS"

A-6A 152584 VMA(AW)-225 departing NAS Willow Grove, Pennsylvania, August 1967. This Intruder was remanufactured as an A-6E and received the SWIP mods. *Picciani*

A-6A 151826 VMA(AW)-225 at an unknown civilian airfield in 1967. It is displayed as a KA-6D at the National Naval Aviation Museum, Pensacola, Florida. *NNAM*

VMA(AW)-242 "BATS"

A-6A 155625 VMA(AW)-242 with the AN/AVQ-10A Precision Avionics Vectoring Equipment (PAVE) KNIFE pod; photographed in 1971, the year the squadron returned from Vietnam. *USN*

152953 was the next-to-last A-6A constructed. It was remanufactured as an A-6E and reassigned to VMA(AW)-242 in 1978. *Grove*

VMA(AW)-332 "POLKA DOTS" / "MOONLIGHTERS"

A-6A 154167 VMA(AW)-332,
February 17, 1973. *Knowles*

A-6E 155583 VMA(AW)-332,
July 1977. *Grove*

VMA(AW)-533 "HAWKS"

A-6A 152640, assigned to VMA(AW)-533 during February 1967. A month later the squadron flew from MCAS Cherry Point, North Carolina, to Chu Lai, South Vietnam, arriving April 1, 1967. *Grove*

VMA(AW)-533 received their first A-6Es during 1976, about the time 159311 was photographed at Luke AFB. *Rotramel*

CHAPTER 9
Combat Operations

A-6As assigned to VA-75 conducting a predeployment training flight. *USN*

Vietnam War

VA-75 "Sunday Punchers"

The "Sunday Punchers" introduced the Intruder to combat in Vietnam during summer 1965, from the deck of USS *Independence* (CVA-62). Initially the squadron flew from Dixie Station, attacking Viet Cong fortifications. The "Indy" then moved north to attack targets in Laos and North Vietnam from Yankee Station. During the next ten days they would lose three Intruders: 151584, 151577, and 151585. All three losses were the result of bomb-fusing issues causing a premature detonation of ordnance. One of these losses, 151577, resulted in the capture of Cmdr. Jeremiah Denton and B/N Lt. (jg) Bill Tshudy. Crews from the other two stricken Intruders were rescued. During a Japanese television interview, while in captivity, Denton blinked out a distress signal using Morse code. As a result he received the Navy Cross. The Sunday Punchers suffered yet another loss when Cmdr. Leonard Vogt and Lt. R. F. Barber were killed on September 17, 1965. Their A-6A, 151588, crashed off Bach Long Island, near Haiphong, while attacking nearby patrol boats. The Intruder's first foray into combat operations ended on November 1, 1965.

After departing San Diego on November 18, 1967, aboard USS *Kitty Hawk* (CVA-63), the "Sunday Punchers" returned to the Gulf of Tonkin for their third Vietnam War cruise, commencing December 5, 1967. This tour resulted in the award of a Navy Cross to Cmdr. Jerrod M. Zacharias and LCmdr. Michael R. Hall for extraordinary heroism on February 24, 1968, during a coordinated low-level night strike carried out against port facilities in the city of Hanoi. The crew experienced and overcame a system discrepancy

A-6A 152913 assigned to VA-75 recovering aboard *Kitty Hawk* following a 1968 sortie over North Vietnam. *USN*

and pressed home their attack despite encountering heavy ground fire and numerous SAM launches. Two A-6As were lost on this cruise: 152917, on December 31, 1967, brought down by a SAM near Vinh, North Vietnam; and 152922, on March 6, 1968, shot down by ground fire near Haiphong. All four crewmembers were killed in action (KIA). *Kitty Hawk* departed Subic Bay on May 28, 1968, en route to her home port of San Diego.

During 1972, USS *Saratoga* (CVA-60), embarking VA-75, kept up an active tempo of operations, flying from Yankee Station. The "Sunday Punchers" laid mines in the waters of the port of Haiphong and struck power plants, storage depots, bridges, and SAM sites. The squadron expended 10 million pounds of ordnance, destroying vehicles, antiaircraft artillery (AAA), and SAM sites, along with almost 300 structures and cratering five runways. This, their final cruise of the Vietnam War, resulted in the loss of three Intruders. A-6A 155626 was lost on September 6, 1972, via a SAM over Haiphong. The pilot was killed and the B/N taken prisoner. The second, on November 28, 1972, involved A-6A 155622 due to a failed launch. The pilot was killed and the B/N rescued. The third loss occurred on December 21, 1972, involving A-6A 152946. It was brought down by ground fire near Kien An Airfield, Haiphong. Both crewmen were KIA. *Saratoga* departed Yankee Station on January 7, 1973.

VA-85 "Black Falcons"

The first deployment of the "Black Falcons" to Vietnam—October 1965 to June 1966—was aboard USS *Kitty Hawk*. Initially they operated off the coast of South Vietnam from Dixie Station. After transitioning north to Yankee Station, VA-85 Intruders effectively used poor weather and the cover of darkness to knock out the Hai Duong bridge and destroy the thermal power plant at Unog Bi. Their first deployment was costly for man and machine. On December 21, 1965, Cmdr. B. J. Cartwright and B/N Lt. Ed Gold were lost during a strike over North Vietnam. They were flying A-6A 151781. On February 18, 1966, BuNo 151797 was brought down while conducting a reconnaissance mission near Hanoi, resulting in the loss of Lt. (jg) Joe Murray and Lt. (jg) Tom Schroeffel. Another loss was suffered on April 17, when BuNo 151794 was hit by ground fire. Fortunately the crew, LCmdr. Sam Sayers and LCmdr. Charles Hawkins, were rescued. An April 27, 1966, mission involving the use of napalm against North Vietnamese barges resulted in the awarding of the Navy Cross to Lt. (jg) Brian E. Westin, who risked his life to save his wounded pilot, Lt. W. R. Westerman. After being pulled to safety by the Search And Rescue (SAR) helicopter, Westin reentered shark-infested waters to ensure Westerman was hoisted to safety. The A-6A flown that date was BuNo 151788. In all six VA-85 Intruders were lost during this cruise.

A-6B Mod 0 151558 VA-75, September 1972, armed with two AGM-78 Standard ARMs in addition to a pair of AGM-45 Shrikes. *Via Davis*

On April 22, 1966, LCmdr. Robert F. Weimorts and Lt. (jg) William B. Nickerson lost their lives while on an armed reconnaissance mission over North Vietnam. They were flying A-6A 151785. *USN*

A-6A 151798 VA-85 was downed by ground fire on April 21, 1966, while on a night mission to attack a heavily defended supply depot near Vinh, North Vietnam. The crew, Capt. Jack E. Keller and Cmdr. Ellis E. Austin, were listed as MIA, later changed to KIA in June 1974. *USN*

BUCKEYE 510 A-6A 151590 was lost on January 19, 1967, after it was hit by AAA while attacking a bridge 6 miles from the Dong Phong Thuong transportation complex, Thanh Hoa Province, North Vietnam. The pilot, Cmdr. Al Brady, ejected and was taken prisoner. The B/N, LCmdr. Bill Yarbrough, was killed when his parachute failed to open. *Via Morgan*

March 25, 1967, VA-85, A-6A 151782, taxies to a catapult aboard *Kitty Hawk,* armed with Mk. 82 Snakeyes. *Moeser*

In December 1966 the squadron was back on Yankee Station, flying once again from *Kitty Hawk*. During this cruise they generated 988 combat sorties, knocking out the North's largest motor vehicle depot, five thermal power plants, the second-largest airbase, and the only steel mill capable of manufacturing steel for railroads and bridges. One notable mission was a daylight "ALPHA STRIKE" on Kep Airfield, northwest of Haiphong, April 24, 1967. SAMs protected the field, along with MiGs and AAA. The latter brought down A-6A 152589, crewed by Lt. (jg) Irv Williams and Lt. (jg) Mike Christian. Williams and Christian were captured and spent seven years as prisoners of war. During this tour, which ended in June 1967, two additional A-6As were lost (151587 and 151590), with four naval aviators taken POW or missing in action (MIA).

A-6A 152948 VA-85, 1968, USS *America*. Of interest is the impressive scoreboard displayed on 154129. *Schrupp*

The "Black Falcons" returned to the Gulf of Tonkin in April 1968 for a third tour, this time aboard USS *America*, and broke existing records by launching 1,448 combat sorties. Two Intruders were lost during this cruise, resulting in the loss of three aircrew KIA or captured. The most notable of these took place on September 6, 1968, when the squadron commander, Cmdr K. L. Coskey, was shot down by ground fire over the Song Ca River near Vinh/Ben Thuy, North Vietnam. Cmdr Coskey was taken prisoner and his B/N, LCmdr. R. G. McKee, was rescued. They were flying BuNo 154127.

For their fourth and final deployment to Vietnam, VA-85 sailed aboard USS *Constellation* (CVA-64), equipped with new A-6A Intruders and two A-6Bs. Once again operating from the Gulf of Tonkin (September 1969 to May 1970), the Black Falcons flew 1,500 sorties and concentrated on interdicting truck traffic. Not a single Intruder was lost on this cruise.

VA-65 "Tigers"

The "Tigers" of VA-65 sailed for Vietnam aboard USS *Constellation* on May 12, 1966, and conducted their first combat sortie on June 15, 1966. On July 1, they took part in the destruction of three North Vietnamese patrol boats observed approaching USS *Coontz*

A-6A 151816 was the first loss suffered by VA-65. It was hit by ground fire while attacking the Hoi Thuong Barracks, North Vietnam, on June 25, 1966. It was forced to ditch, with the loss of the B/N, Lt. (jg) Charles W. Marik. The pilot, LCmdr. Richard M. Weber, was rescued. *USN*

On August 27, 1966, A-6A 151822 was brought down by ground fire near Vinh, resulting in the capture of crew members LCmdr. John H. Fellowes and Lt. (jg) George T. Coker. *USN*

A-6A 151817, loaded with eighteen Mk. 82 Snakeyes, about to be launched on a mission sometime in 1966. *Via Morgan*

(DLG-9) at high speed. Between October 25 and 31, as a result of poor weather, the squadron flew 37 percent of all Yankee Station sorties into North Vietnam. There were two Intruders lost in combat operations; both wore an experimental green camouflage scheme.

During their second combat cruise VA-65 embarked aboard USS *Forrestal* (CVA-59). The "Black Falcons" were only on station five days when a fire broke out on the flight deck on July 29, 1967. VA-65 personnel were among the 134 sailors killed with 161 injured. The fire caused extensive damage, resulting in *Forrestal*'s departure from Yankee Station. The "Black Falcons" sent a detachment of Intruders (Det-64) to USS *Constellation* to augment VA-196 for the remainder of that ship's 1967 cruise.

The "Black Falcons" final Vietnam War cruise was aboard USS *Kitty Hawk* from December 30, 1968, to September 4, 1969. *Kitty Hawk*, with VA-65 aboard, departed Yankee Station and relieved USS *Enterprise* (CVAN-65) in the Sea of Japan. This redeployment was due to North Korea downing a Navy EC-121M on April 15, 1969. The squadron returned to flying combat sorties for the remainder of the cruise. One A-6A (155587) was lost on April 3, 1969, when it was shot down while attacking a fuel storage area near Ban Sang/Mu Gia Pass, Khammouan Province, Laos. The crew, LCmdr. Ed Redden and Lt. John Ricci, were rescued.

A-6A 152595 VMA(AW)-242, Da Nang 1967. This Intruder was destroyed on the ground during a Viet Cong rocket attack on July 27, 1968. *USN*

Marine Cpl. Robert D. Lynam, an ordnanceman with VMA(AW)-242, chalks up a 1968 bomb tally on a 500-pound bomb hung from A-6A 152604. *USMC*

Vietnam War–era VMA(AW)-242 "Batmen" patch. *Author's collection*

VMA(AW)-242 "Bats"

In late 1966, VMA(AW)-242 joined the 1st Marine Aircraft Wing (MAW) at Da Nang Air Base, Republic of Vietnam, becoming the first Marine Intruder squadron deployed to Vietnam. By November they were participating in combat operations against the Viet Cong and the People's Army of Vietnam. Initially the squadron supported allied ground forces, but during April 1967, they were also assigned the first of many Rolling Thunder missions over North Vietnam. The squadron flew sorties over North Vietnam until the bombing halt in late 1968. Until the squadron departed from Vietnam in late April 1971 the "Bats" continued supporting allied forces in South Vietnam, as well as flying sorties against the Ho Chi Minh Trail, Vietnam, and central Laos. Maj. Fred J. Cone and Lt. Col. Lewis H. Abrams received the Navy Cross for actions while attacking Phuc Yen Air Base near Hanoi on October 25, 1967. After successfully evading four SAMs they were able to contribute 4.5 tons of ordnance to cratering runways there. While egressing the target area they encountered and outmaneuvered a fifth SAM. VMA(AW)-242 returned to MCAS El Toro, California, on September 12, 1970.

A-6A 154133 VA-52 photographed during 1969, between Vietnam War cruises. Of interest is the row of bomb symbols visible under the wing. *NNAM*

VA-52 "Knightriders"

When the "Knightriders" of VA-52 embarked aboard USS *Coral Sea* (CVA-43), they were the first Intruder squadron to deploy aboard a Midway-class carrier. The unit lost one Intruder on this cruise, A-6A 154141, on October 13, 1968. While returning from a mission over North Vietnam, it suddenly disappeared from tracking radar near the mouth of the Song Kanh Can River, southeast of Vinh. The crew, Cmdr. Quinlen R. Orell and Lt. James D. Hunt, were KIA. The Intruder and its crew were never found.

The "Knightriders" returned to the waters off Vietnam on December 8, 1970, embarked aboard USS *Kitty Hawk*. The squadron, equipped with a mix of A-6A and A-6B Intruders, concentrated on transportation targets and lines of communication in Laos until departing for home on June 23, 1971.

Due to the North Vietnamese Spring Offensive of the South on March 30, 1972, operations began a few days earlier than planned on April 3, with the most-significant strikes into North Vietnam since October 1968. This operation became known as Freedom Train. Operation Freedom Porch followed with attacks on Haiphong, Thanh Hoa, and Vinh. VA-52 also played a crucial role in Operation Pocket Money, the mining of Haiphong harbor.

PAT/ARM A-6B 155628, assigned to VA-52 en route to a target in North Vietnam 1970. *USN*

The "Knightriders" took part in Operation Linebacker, May 9–October 23, 1972, with concentrated attacks above the twentieth parallel. These included Alpha strikes, mine seeding, tanker operations, standard ARM sorties against SAM sites, armed reconnaissance, and Sneaky Pete missions—nighttime sorties involving single Intruders.

On August 20, 1972, A-6A 157018 was flying a low-level transportation interdiction sortie when a SAM downed it near the village of Ky Thuong. The crew, Lt. R. Barnum and Lt. Harry S. Mossman, were initially listed as MIA. This finding was later updated to KIA. The wreckage was eventually located in 1997 on Cu Xu Island, North Vietnam.

In November 1973, VA-52 deployed on its final Vietnam War deployment. Once again it was aboard USS *Kitty Hawk*. This cruise marked the first time all aspects of carrier aviation warfare were consolidated into one air wing.

VA-52 shoulder patch. *Author*

A-6A 157020 assigned to VA-52 parked on the ramp at Hill AFB, February 3, 1973. *Knowles*

A-6A 152906 launching from USS *Ranger* on a mission to strike a target in North Vietnam from Yankee Station, December 14, 1967. *USN*

VA-165 "Boomers"

VA-165 was the first operational West Coast Intruder squadron to fly combat missions over Vietnam. They arrived in the waters off Vietnam on December 3, 1967, aboard USS *Ranger* (CVA-61). The "Boomers" participated in strikes against bridges, airfields, transportation hubs, SAM, and AAA sites. On January 23, A-6A 152932 impacted the sea during a low-level ingress while attacking the Ha Duong Military Complex 4 miles southeast of Hanoi. Cmdr. Leland S. Kollmorgen ejected and was rescued. LCmdr. Gerald L Ramsden remained with the aircraft, and his body was not recovered. On January 26, 1968, two additional Boomers, LCmdr. Norman E. Eidsmore and Lt. Michael E. Dunn, were lost in the crash of A-6A 152901. They were in the process of attacking the airfield at Vinh when all radio contact was lost. Both crew members were listed as MIA, later changed to KIA.

Due to North Korea's capture of USS *Pueblo* (AGER-2) on January 23, 1968, *Ranger* was ordered to the Sea of Japan and operated there until relieved on March 5, 1968. *Ranger* returned to Yankee Station and began combat operations later in March. A total of four Navy Crosses would be awarded for those March missions. On March 24, Lt. James W. Pate Jr. and Lt. Roger W.

VA-165, A-6A 155605 photographed hauling five triple ejector racks loaded with Mk. 82 500-pound bombs. This Intruder was written off on February 28, 1970, when it caught fire during launch from USS *Ranger*. The crew, Lt. R. R. Wittenberg and Lt. H. W. Paul, were rescued by the SAR helicopter. *Anderson*

A-6C 155662 VA-165 July 1970. The "Boomers" were the first Intruder squadron to deploy TRIM in combat. *Inoue*

Krueger flew a mission against a heavily defended and strategically vital railroad yard at Kinh No, in northeast North Vietnam. Despite intense ground fire and a barrage of SAMs Pate and Krueger pressed home their attack, destroying the target. On March 30, while flying a single Intruder night attack mission against a heavily defended port facility near Hanoi, the crew of LCmdr. Robert M. McEwen and LCmdr. Gerald W. Rogers pressed home their attack despite experiencing difficulties with their inertial navigation system, in the process evading four SAMs and intense radar-directed AAA fire to deliver their bombs on target. On May 13, 1968, USS *Ranger* departed NAS Cubi Point, Philippines, bound for NAS Alameda, California.

USS *Ranger*, embarking VA-165, once again deployed to the Gulf of Tonkin, arriving on November 29, 1968. The "Boomers" spent two extended periods of combat operations flying from Yankee Station. However, when a pair of North Korean MiGs shot down an unarmed EC-121M reconnaissance aircraft on April 15, 1969, USS *Ranger* became part of Task Force 71, moving to the Sea of Japan until May 5, when it departed for its home port of Alameda, California.

VA-165 returned to the Gulf of Tonkin on May 26, 1970, aboard USS *America* and immediately began launching aircraft on combat missions from Yankee Station. Cmdr. Fred M. Backman, the "Boomers'" commanding officer, with B/N LCmdr. Jack Hawley flew the first combat sortie operating the new A-6C TRIM Intruder. *America* and VA-165 spent 100 days on Yankee Station, attacking transportation hubs, storage facilities, bridges, and waterborne logistics craft. On November 7, *America* cruised for home, with VA-165 completing its fifth combat deployment to Southeast Asia.

USS *Constellation* and VA-165 arrived on Yankee Station late in 1971 and immediately commenced airstrikes against targets in Laos. To counter MiG incursions into Laos, the USAF and Navy combined to suppress this MiG threat via coordinated attacks from December 26 to 30. The primary targets assigned to the Navy were Dong Hoi, Quang Khe, and Vinh. "*Connie's*" tour was extended to provide additional firepower to turn the tide of the Easter Offensive, the North's invasion of South Vietnam. Beginning April 5, 1972, the "Boomers" participated in Operation Freedom Train, tactical airstrikes into North Vietnam targeting logistics. Freedom Train became Operation Linebacker on April 10. These

A-6A 155699 photographed April 25, 1972, aboard USS *Constellation* during combat flight operations on Yankee Station. Of interest is the load of 500-pound Mk. 82s with conical fin assemblies (CFA). *Reichwein*

strikes amounted to the first sustained bombing of the North since 1968. Operation Freedom Porch began April 16, with Intruders striking targets in and around Haiphong.

Between April 25 and 30, aircraft from VA-165 supported South Vietnamese troops by hitting targets around An Loc, including artillery, tanks, bunkers, and troop concentrations only 40 miles from Saigon. Following 154 days off the coast of Vietnam, *Constellation* departed for San Francisco on July 1, 1972. This nine-month deployment saw seven aircraft lost, two aircrew KIA, and two taken prisoner. One of those aircraft lost was A-6A 155677, on December 30, 1971. Struck by a SAM, 155677 broke apart over the Gulf of Tonkin near Hon Nieu Island, North Vietnam. The crew, LCmdr. Frederick L. Holmes and Lt. Burton, ejected from their stricken craft. A SAR helicopter rescued Lt. Burton, but LCmdr. Holmes was listed as MIA and later changed to KIA in 1975.

On January 5, 1973, USS *Constellation* began her seventh deployment to Vietnam; it would also be the seventh Vietnam War cruise for the "Boomers" of VA-165. The Vietnam War ceasefire took effect on January 27, 1973. Combat missions continued to be flown from Yankee Station into Laos after that country requested assistance. "Connie" returned to home port on October 11, 1973. After almost ten years of intensive combat operations, the last Intruder squadron deployed in support of the Vietnam War came home.

VA-196 "Main Battery"

During 1967, USS *Constellation* made her third deployment to Vietnam. During this eight-month deployment, VA-196 would lose three Intruders in one day when A-6As 152625, 152627, and 152638 were downed on a daylight raid against Duc Noi railroad yards north of Hanoi on August 21, 1967. A-6A 152638 was struck by ground fire or a SAM while making its bombing run, forcing the crew, Cmdr. Leo T. Profilet and Cmdr. William M. Hardman, to eject. They were captured and taken POW. A-6As 152625 and 152627 dodged intense ground fire, including numerous SAMs, as they egressed the target. Adverse weather forced the pair farther north than planned. Airborne early warning aircraft tracked the flight crossing into Chinese airspace with MiGs in pursuit. Peking radio later reported downing two aircraft that had violated their airspace. Cmdr. Jimmy L. Buckley, the pilot of 152625, was KIA; LCmdr. Robert Flynn was captured and held prisoner in China

Undated photo of A-6B (Mod 0) 151562 assigned to VA-196. *Jacobs*

until 1973. Lt. (jg) J. Forrest Trembley and Lt. (jg) Dain V. Scott, flying 152627, were listed as MIA and later updated to KIA.

On October 30, 1967, Cmdr. Charles B. Hunter and Lt. Lyle F. Bull flew a perfectly planned and executed single-plane, night, radar bombing mission on a heavily defended Hanoi railroad ferry dock. The entire local air defense system focused on this lone Intruder, and at one point six SAMs were tracking the lone attacker. Despite this the crew pressed on with their attack and released ordnance on target with extreme accuracy. The crew then egressed the target area under intense ground fire, including the launch of four additional SAMs. For their actions Cmdr. Hunter and Lt. Bull were awarded the Navy Cross.

A-6A 152629 launched on a night mission on November 2, 1967, to attack the ferry at Kim Quan, south of Hanoi. Radar and radio contact were lost while the Intruder was engaged in a night low-level bombing run. The crew, LCmdr. Richard D. Morrow and Lt. James J. Wright, were listed as MIA. Following the release of American POWs in February 1973, their status was updated to KIA.

A-6A 154155 VA-196 loaded with sixteen Mk. 82 Snakeyes aboard *Constellation* in October 1968, just weeks before President Johnson's halt to the bombing of North Vietnam. *USN*

USS *Constellation* began her fourth deployment to Vietnam on May 29, 1968. On November 1, President Lyndon B. Johnson directed all bombing of North Vietnam to be halted at 2100 hours Saigon time. "*Connie*" returned home on January 31, 1969, after supporting more than 11,000 combat and support missions and dropping almost 20,000 tons of ordnance. Three aircraft were lost, including A-6B (Mod 0) 151560 on August 20, 1968. Shortly after launch it suffered a wing slat failure. As a result the pilot was unable to maintain control of the aircraft. The crew, Lt. (jg) D.C. Brandenstein and Lt. W. A. Neal, ejected and were rescued.

A-6A 154149 was downed September 30, 1968, possibly by a SAM during a night armed reconnaissance mission near Yen Thanh, north of Vinh, Nghe An Province, North Vietnam. Both crew members, Lt. (jg) Larry Jack Van Renselaar and Lt. Domenick Anthony Spinelli, were initially listed as MIA and later confirmed as KIA.

During the next cruise (October 14, 1969, to June 1, 1970), USS *Ranger* spent two extended periods on Yankee Station, the longest being forty-five days. On November 22, 1969, A-6A 155613 suffered a wing failure during a mission near Tavouac, 15 miles south of the Ashau Valley, Laos. The crew, Cmdr. Lloyd W Richards and Lt. (jg) Richard Carl Deuter, ejected. Unfortunately Lt. Deuter was killed; Cmdr. Richards was rescued by a USAF HH-53 Jolly Green Giant and flown to Da Nang.

A-6A 154150 was lost on December 18, 1968. One possible cause was listed as a premature detonation of the Intruder's ordnance during a daylight Steel Tiger strike in Laos. Lt. (jg) John R. Babcock and Lt. Gary J. Meyer were listed as MIA, later confirmed KIA. *USN*

A-6A 152937 was shot down by AAA on January 2, 1970, during a strike against a storage dump near Ban Na Phao / Mu Gia Pass, Khammouan Province, Laos. The crew, LCmdr. Nicholas G. Brooks and Lt. Bruce C. Fryar, ejected, but their fates, although listed as KIA, are somewhat of a mystery. They were initially listed as MIA; their status was later updated to KIA. LCmdr. Brooks's remains were repatriated in 1982. Lt. Fryar's remains have yet to be located.

On February 6, 1970, A-6A 155618 was hit by AAA while attacking trucks on a Steel Tiger mission near Ban Kapay, Laos. The crew, LCmdr. Evan P. Reese and Lt. (jg) D. R. Fraser, ejected. The crew was rescued the following day by a USAF HH-53 Jolly Green Giant.

A-6A 155607 was lost November 22, 1969, while flying a night armed reconnaissance mission over the Ho Chi Minh Trail. The Intruder came down 25 miles southwest of Khe Sanh. The precise cause of the crash is unknown. The crew, LCmdr. Dick Collins and Lt. Mike Quinn, were both listed as MIA, updated to KIA in 1978.

On July 16, 1971, VA-196 arrived off the coast of Vietnam aboard USS *Enterprise* and immediately commenced combat operations. KA-6D 152590 suffered instrument malfunctions, resulting in the Intruder stalling upon launch on October 9, 1971, and going into the Gulf of Tonkin. The crew was recovered. On December 18, 1972, President Richard M. Nixon ordered the renewed bombing of North Vietnam north of the twentieth parallel. This new aerial campaign became known as Freedom Train. Missions included the remining of Haiphong harbor and concentrated airstrikes against antiaircraft sites, army barracks, storage facilities, rail and shipyards, and transportation hubs. Most Navy sorties were concentrated in the coastal areas around Hanoi and Haiphong. Between December 18 and 22 the Big "E" was joined by *Saratoga*, *Oriskany*, *America*, and *Ranger*. All further combat missions were canceled on January 27, 1973.

However, a request for assistance by the Laotian government resulted in additional combat sorties being flown into Laos on the twenty-eighth. Operation End Sweep, flown from March 10 to April 6, was a mine-clearing operation in Haiphong harbor. It was during the 1972–73 cruise that VA-196 experimented with an in-cockpit laser designator, Northrop's AN/AVQ-27 Laser Target Designation System (LTDS), believed to be the only Intruder squadron to employ this device. It was used successfully to illuminate targets for A-7E Corsairs.

The "Main Battery" suffered one combat loss during this cruise when A-6A 155594 was hit by ground fire over Haiphong the night of December 20, 1972. Cmdr. Gordon Nakagawa and Lt. Ken H.

Higdon ejected. Both were captured upon hitting the ground. A-6A 155594 would be the last VA-196 Intruder lost in Vietnam.

VMA(AW)-224 “Bengals”

In December 1971, the “Bengals” arrived in the South China Sea aboard USS *Coral Sea*. The squadron took part in Operation Proud Deep Alpha, the largest US bombing campaign since the end of Rolling Thunder. Operation Freedom Train followed, countering the North’s invasion of South Vietnam. Freedom Train took the air war back across the twentieth parallel for the first time since 1968. Strikes in North Vietnam were against vehicle targets, lines of communication (roads, waterways, bridges, railroad bridges, and railroad tracks), resupply, air defense, and industrial / power generation targets.

The “Bengals” were the only carrier deployed Marine Intruder squadron of the war and would complete six line periods on Yankee Station. Their most notable mission was Operation Pocket Money, the historic mining of Haiphong harbor begun on May 8, 1972. USS *Coral Sea* dispatched three A-6As carrying four Mk. 52-2 mines each. The targets were the outer approaches to Haiphong harbor. The mining aircraft timed their departure from *Coral Sea* to execute the mining at precisely the same time President Nixon publicly announced the operation. This flight, led by Cmdr. Roger E. Sheets, was composed of Navy and Marine Corps Intruders. The mines were set with seventy-two-hour arming delays, thus permitting merchant ships time to depart or change their destination consistent with the president’s public warning. This operation was phase one of a campaign that seeded more than 11,000 500-pound Mk. 36–type Destructor (DST) mines and 108 1,200-pound Mk. 52-2 bottom mines. The mission proved instrumental in compelling North Vietnam to negotiate an end to the war.

VMA(AW)-224 became the only Marine Intruder squadron to deploy aboard an aircraft carrier during the Vietnam War when they embarked aboard USS *Coral Sea* for one cruise from March 9 to November 8, 1973. *USN*

A-6A 155654 assigned to VMA(AW)-224 prepares to launch from USS *Coral Sea*, loaded with Mk. 52-2 bottom mines for Haiphong harbor, May 8, 1972. *Albrecht*

A-6A 155655 VMA(AW)-224, June 21, 1972, USS *Coral Sea*, with hastily applied nose art and mission markings. *Wada*

VA-35 "Black Panthers"

USS *Enterprise*, with VA-35 embarked, arrived on Yankee Station on December 18, 1966. Noteworthy missions included the seeding of Mk. 55 and Mk. 52-2 bottom mines in the Song Ca and Song Giang Rivers, North Vietnam, the first such aerial mining since World War II. On May 19, 1967, A-6A 152594 was lost when struck by a SAM during an Alpha Strike on the Van Dien depot near Hanoi. The crew, LCmdr. Eugene B. McDaniel and Lt. J. K. Patterson, ejected and were taken prisoner. LCmdr. McDaniel would later receive the Navy Cross for extraordinary heroism as a POW in North Vietnam. *Enterprise* departed the Gulf of Tonkin for Alameda, California, on June 20, 1967.

The "Black Panthers" once again sailed aboard the Big "E" for their second Vietnam cruise from January 3, 1968, to July 18, 1968. While visiting Sasebo, *Enterprise* was ordered to the Sea of Japan in response to the seizure of USS *Pueblo* (AGER-2) by North Korea. The carrier and her escorts were released on February 16 and returned to Yankee Station. The first Intruder lost on this cruise was 152938 on February 28, 1968. The crew, LCmdr. Henry Coons and Lt. Tom Stegman, were inbound to attack the North Vietnamese airfield at Bai Thong when radio contact was lost. A search for the aircraft and missing crew recovered only aircraft parts, including a flak-damaged vertical stabilizer.

Cmdr. Glenn E. Kollmann and Lt. John G. Griffith were awarded the Navy Cross for a night mission flown on February 24, 1968. The target was a heavily defended port described as being in the heart of North Vietnam. Despite monsoon-like weather conditions and heavy ground fire, including surface-to-air missiles, the crew successfully penetrated the target's defenses, delivering the ordnance on target and "inflicting substantial damage upon the port facilities." This crew perished the night of March 12, when their A-6A, 152943, crashed into the gulf after launching from *Enterprise*. The last transmission recorded was "rolling, rolling, eject, eject, ejecting." Despite an intensive search, neither crew member was recovered. As a result their Navy Crosses were awarded posthumously.

On March 16, 1968, A-6A 152940 was attacking the railway yard at Khe Nu, Yen Bai Province, North Vietnam, when it was shot down by ground fire. The crew, LCmdr. Edwin A. Shuman and LCmdr. Dale W. Doss, ejected and were taken prisoner. This fact was confirmed the following day by Hanoi radio. Both were released on March 14, 1973.

On May 13, 1968, while attacking Vinh airfield, A-6A 152951 was struck by a 37 mm round. Fragments entered the cockpit, injuring the pilot, Lt. Bruce B. Bremner. The crew still managed to deliver their ordnance on target, a load of Mk. 36 mines. While egressing the target a fire broke out, followed by an explosion that forced the crew to eject. Bremer and Lt. J. T. Fardy were picked up by a UH-2 Seasprite SAR helicopter and returned to *Enterprise*. A-6A 152949 was lost on June 24, 1968, when hit by AAA while mining a waterway with Mk. 36 mines, 5 miles from Vinh, North Vietnam. The primary target for this mission was the Kim Ma interdiction point on the Song Ca River near Vinh. Other crews witnessed a fireball followed by an emergency beeper. Lt. Nicholas M. Carpenter and Lt. Joseph Scott Mobley ejected. Carpenter was killed; Mobley survived and was taken prisoner. 152949 would become the last Intruder lost during this cruise. The Big "E" departed Cubi Point, Philippines, for Alameda, California, on July 7, 1968.

The "Black Panthers" returned to the Gulf of Tonkin aboard USS *Coral Sea*. This cruise marked *Coral Sea*'s fifth deployment and VA-35's third. During five line periods from October 27, 1969, to June 1, 1970, VA-35 would lose only one Intruder, A-6A 152891. The loss occurred on December 26, 1969, 110 miles off the coast of Vietnam. A crippled Intruder was on approach to the carrier. When only 300 yards from the ship, it suddenly nose-dived into the water. Both crew members, Lt.(jg) Walter H. Kosky and Lt. (jg) Dustin C. Trowbridge, ejected, but their parachutes did not have time to deploy and both were killed. Only Kosky's body was recovered.

A full-color view of A-6A 152939, assigned to VA-35, armed with Mk. 36 DST mines, 1968. *Schrupp*

A-6A 151806 assigned to VA-35 aboard *Coral Sea* being directed to the catapult April 31, 1970. *USN*

The fourth and final Vietnam deployment for VA-35 was aboard USS *America*, with the first line period commencing July 17, 1972. In all, seven line periods of intense action followed, involving VA-35 flying missions into North and South Vietnam, including Linebacker II, December 18–29, 1972. Two Intruders were lost on this cruise. The first, 157028, was brought down by AAA on September 17, 1972, while flying an armed reconnaissance sortie in the Haiphong / Hai Doung area of North Vietnam. The crew, Cmdr. Verne Donnelly and LCmdr. Ken Buell, were initially listed as MIA and later changed to KIA. Cmdr. Donnelly's remains were recovered and positively identified in 1991.

The Black Panthers had the dubious honor of losing the last Intruder of the Vietnam War when A-6A 157007 was brought down by antiaircraft fire on January 24, 1973. The crew, Lt. C. M. Graf and Lt. S. H. Hatfield, were providing close air support near Quang Tri, South Vietnam, when a SAM or 37 mm AAA hit their Intruder. Graf was able to fly the crippled jet out to sea, where they ejected and were rescued by a Navy helicopter. With their final line period completed, VA-35 and *America* sailed for home, arriving on March 24, 1973.

A-6A assigned to VA-35, adding additional bomb tonnage during Linebacker II. *Schrupp*

VA-95 "Green Lizards"

The "Green Lizards" made one Intruder cruise to the waters off North Vietnam from April through October 1973. Embarked aboard USS *Coral Sea* with a full complement of A-6A/B and KA-6Ds, VA-95 participated in Operation End Sweep, the clearing of mines near Haiphong. No Intruders were lost during this cruise.

The unit returned to the western Pacific—once again aboard *Coral Sea*—from December 1974 to July 1975. VA-95 flew armed escort missions in support of Operation Frequent Wind, the evacuation of Saigon.

A-6A 154144 about to launch from USS *Coral Sea* in 1973. This Intruder crashed into the Mediterranean Sea with the loss of both crew on May 22, 1983. *Cook*

A-6B 151558, assigned to VA-95, received the A-6B Mod 0 conversion in 1968. It was photographed in 1974 and was most likely designated a Mod 0/1. *USN*

Delivered June 2, 1967, as an A-6A, 152921 was modified by Grumman to KA-6D configuration. It is seen here assigned to VA-95 during 1973. *USN*

VA-115 "Arabs"

USS *Midway* (CVA-41) arrived on Yankee Station on May 18, 1971. VA-115 supported interdiction operations along the DMZ, Laos, and Cambodia until returning to home port on October 31.

In April 1972, USS *Midway*, with VA-115 embarked, departed NAS Alameda, California, en route to Yankee Station. The squadron supported Linebacker operations primarily in North Vietnam, including day and night interdiction and strike missions, as well as Alpha Strikes. It also participated in the first three days of the Linebacker II "Christmas Bombing" campaign.

The Arabs lost 155693 on January 9, 1973, when it crashed south of Kan Ty, Nghe An Province, North Vietnam. In addition to AAA fire, an estimated fifteen SAMs were fired at the strike force. The crew, Lt. Michael T. McCormick and Lt. (jg) Robert Clark, were initially posted as MIA. The secretary of the Navy approved Presumptive Findings of Death for McCormick on July 25, 1975, and for Clark on March 7, 1978. Mike McCormick and Robert Clark were the last of seven VA-115 aircrews lost during the Vietnam War.

During this cruise, VA-115 introduced the KA-6D to combat operations. This example, KA-6D 151824, was photographed during 1975. *Wada*

A-6A 155692, assigned to VA-115, photographed during May–June 1972. *Author's collection*

A-6A 156995 assigned to VA-115, May 6, 1973. *Author's collection*

A-6A 155711, assigned to VA-115, circa 1973 with a Ford Aeronutronic AN/AVQ-10A PAVE KNIFE laser designation pod mounted on the centerline. Only three A-6A Intruders were modified for the carriage of PAVE KNIFE pods. *Lawson*

USS *Midway*, embarking VA-115, departed Alameda on September 11, 1973, to make Yokosuka, Japan, their home port. During this tour VA-115 operated from NAF Atsugi. On April 19, 1975, *Midway* was dispatched to the coast of Vietnam to participate in Operation Eagle Pull, the evacuation of Phnom Penh, Cambodia, and again in April for Operation Frequent Wind, the evacuation of Saigon.

VA-145 "Swordsmen"

The "Swordsmen" of VA-145 returned to the waters off Southeast Asia embarked aboard USS *Enterprise* for their fourth combat deployment during winter 1969. The previous three combat tours were completed while operating the venerable A-1H/J Skyraider. This time the squadron was equipped with A-6A/B Intruders. On April 16, 1969, the Big "E" departed Yankee Station en route to a new assignment: Defender Station, off the coast of Korea. This move was in response to the downing of an EC-121M by North Korea on April 15. *Enterprise* would remain on station in the Yellow Sea until May 11, 1969.

A-6A 155704 VA-115 NAS Atsugi, Japan, February 24, 1975. This Intruder received the A-6E and TRAM upgrades. It has the dubious distinction of being accidentally shot down on June 4, 1996, by the Phalanx system of the JDS Yugiri (DD-153). The crew was recovered. *Wada*

A-6C 155660 assigned to VA-145 about to launch from *Ranger*, March 6, 1971. *USN*

A-6A 155715 displays a typical combat configuration AN/AVQ-10A on the centerline hardpoint, with Mk. 82 LGBs (with the fin and wing extensions) inboard and conical-finned NTP Mk. 82s on the outboard MERs. *USN*

AN/AVQ-10A PAVE KNIFE pod mounted on the centerline of an A-6A Intruder. *USN*

A-6B Mod 0/1 149949, assigned to VA-145, at NAS Fallon, Nevada, December 1973, following the "Swordsmen"'s sixth and final cruise to Vietnam. *Jacobs*

VA-145 returned to the Gulf of Tonkin in November 1970, this time embarked aboard USS *Ranger*. The squadron was now equipped with the A-6A and the new A-6C. Two Intruders were lost on this cruise: A-6C 155647 and A-6A 156994. Both losses occurred during catapult launches.

The squadron's sixth and final combat cruise to Vietnam was once again aboard USS *Ranger*. The tour was highlighted by the introduction of the PAVE KNIFE laser-guided bombing system. The AN/AVQ-10A PAVE KNIFE played a key role in the destruction of fourteen highway and railroad bridges in North Vietnam in only three hours during a massive strike on January 20, 1973. This attack was the last Navy bombing mission against North Vietnam. This significant strike capability brought recognition to the Navy's use of the PAVE KNIFE weapons system in a limited war environment. Following the ceasefire, on January 27 VA-145 flew concentrated strikes against targets in Laos. Operation End Sweep mine sweeping missions followed between February and March 1973. *Ranger* returned to Alameda in June 1973.

VMA(AW)-533 "Hawks"

VMA (AW)-533 arrived at Chu Lai, South Vietnam, on April 1, 1967, with 12 A-6A Intruders and fifteen flight crews. The squadron was tasked with generating twelve sorties a night: four over the DMZ and eight into North Vietnam. Sorties were later increased to twelve nocturnal sorties into North Vietnam and four daylight sorties in support of Marine infantry. Targets ranged from south of the DMZ to Hanoi and Haiphong, the majority being heavily defended by SAMs and various-caliber AAA. One such heavily defended target was the Paul Doumer Bridge spanning the Red River. After the USAF dropped the bridge on October 27, 1967, the "Hawks" went in under cover of darkness and seeded the area around the bridge pillars with Mk. 36 Destructor Mines.

They lost their first Intruder, A-6A 152639, on August 26, 1967, when it was downed by ground fire near Ho Gai, North Vietnam. The crew perished in the crash. They would lose two more Intruders: 152636 on January 18, 1968, to ground fire, and 152644 on February 24, 1968, brought down by a SAM. Of those crews, two were KIA and two became POWs. By the end of their

A-6A 152642 was delivered on December 15, 1966, and photographed a year later assigned to VMA(AW)-533. *MacSorley*

A-6A 155679 assigned to VMA(AW)-533. In 1972, the "Hawks" returned to Vietnam, deploying to Nam Phong RTAFB, Thailand. From there they flew combat missions into Cambodia and Laos. In September 1973, the squadron returned to MCAS Iwakuni, Japan, where they would remain until returning to MCAS Cherry Point, North Carolina, November 1975. *Nishimura*

thirteen-month tour they had flown more than 10,000 combat sorties and witnessed one pilot, Maj. Kent C. Bateman, receive the Navy Cross for an October 25, 1967, attack on Phuc Yen Airfield near Hanoi. VMA(AW)-533 left Chu Lai for MCAS Iwakuni on October 5, 1969.

VMA(AW)-225 "Vikings"

The "Vikings" of VMA(AW)-225 arrived at Da Nang Air Base, Republic of Vietnam, on February 5, 1969, joining the Bats of VMA(AW)-242. With the suspension of Rolling Thunder, their primary mission involved close and direct air support for allied ground elements in the I Corps area of South Vietnam. The squadron attacked and destroyed surface targets day and night, and in all weather conditions. A secondary mission was to utilize the Intruder's unique AMTI feature to interdict truck traffic on the Ho Chi Minh Trail. On April 28, 1971, the last Marine in-country Intruder squadron, VMA(AW)-225, returned to MCAS El Toro, California. The squadron was deactivated on June 15, 1972.

A-6A 149944 VMA(AW)-225, May 30, 1967. *NNAM*

A-6A 155609 VMA(AW)-225 Cherry Point, September 6, 1968, just months before deploying to Da Nang Air Base, Republic of Vietnam. *Kasulka*

Cambodia

SS *Mayaguez* Incident

SS *Mayaguez* was a container ship loaded with military equipment, including material from the US Embassy in Saigon. On May 12, 1975, it was seized by Khmer Rouge patrol boats in disputed waters off the coast of Cambodia. USS *Coral Sea* and other combatants, fresh from supporting Operation Frequent Wind, were ordered to proceed at high speed to assist SS *Mayaguez*, arriving May 15, 1975. A force of US Marines embarked aboard USS *Harold E. Holt* (FF-1074) to recapture *Mayaguez*. A second Marine force sent to rescue the crew encountered stiff resistance on the island of Koh Tang and was forced to withdraw.

A-6A Intruders assigned to VA-95 launched from *Coral Sea* at 0700 on an armed reconnaissance mission. This sortie was followed an hour later by two additional Intruders, A-6As 157019 and 157025. Once airborne, they were redirected to attack Ream Field. The pair dropped Mk. 20 Rockeye II CBUs on their first pass, followed by Mk. 82s to crater the runway. A second strike was launched at 1020 hours and destroyed a military barracks. One final mission was called on to provide support for the

A-6A 157023 assigned to VA-95 and photographed October 4, 1975. This Intruder displays the name of Lt. Steve Richmond. Lt. Richmond flew A-6A 157019 on a May 15, 1975, strike against Ream Field, Cambodia. *Logan*

evacuation of the ground forces on Koh Tang Island. This event launched at 1145 hours and was back aboard *Coral Sea* by 1335 hours. The crew of SS *Mayaguez* was freed ten minutes before the start of the third strike.

Iran

Operation Eagle Claw

Operation Eagle Claw was the aborted April 1980 mission to free US Embassy staff held hostage in Tehran, Iran. The US Navy deployed two aircraft carriers, USS *Nimitz* (CVN-68) and USS *Coral Sea*. The combined force included two Intruder squadrons: VA-196 aboard *Coral Sea* and VA-35 aboard *Nimitz*. To distinguish US aircraft from Iranian aircraft, distinctive markings were applied. US Navy F-4 Phantom IIs and F-14 Tomcats had red or yellow stripes applied with a black border. Attack aircraft (A-6s and A-7s) used an orange stripe with black borders. Mechanical failures involving several of the mission's helicopters led to President Jimmy Carter aborting the mission before any strikes into Iran could be launched.

A-6E 154137 VA-196, April 1980, USS *Coral Sea*. *USN*

Grenada

Operation Urgent Fury

Knowing the strategic value of Grenada, the Cuban government began storing arms and military equipment on the 133-square-mile island. Other Caribbean nations sounded the alarm and requested assistance from the United States. Grenada was also home to an American medical school with students in attendance. This further complicated and added a degree of urgency to the invasion. A coalition of six Caribbean nations plus the United States attacked the country before dawn on October 25, 1983. USS *Independence*, with VA-176 embarked, was positioned offshore in the vicinity of St. George as part of Task Group 20-5. During the roughly weeklong conflict, Thunderbolt Intruders provided close air support and aerial refueling.

A-6E 155718 VA-35, April 1980, USS *Nimitz*. *USN*

KA-6D 154133 VA-176, during Operation Urgent Fury. *USN*

Lebanon Crisis

While supporting the Multinational Force in Lebanon, on December 3, 1983, two F-14As were forced to evade SAMs and AAA fire from Syrian-held positions near Hammana, Lebanon. As a result, USS *Independence* and USS *John F. Kennedy* were ordered to execute a retaliatory strike on December 4, 1983. With a scant four hours to prepare, *Independence* launched five VA-176 Intruders, and *Kennedy*, embarking VA-75 and VA-85, contributed twelve. One Intruder, 152915, assigned to VA-85, was shot down by a Syrian missile, most likely a Strela-1 or Strela-2 infrared guided SAM. It crashed near Kfar Salwan, 15 miles east of Beirut. The crew, Lt. Mark "Doppler" Lange and Lt. Robert "Bobby" Goodman, were able to eject; unfortunately Lange died from his injuries. Goodman was captured and held as a POW until released on January 3, 1984.

Two A-6E Intruders assigned to VA-85 and three A-7E Corsair IIs of VA-81 and VA-83 working up at NAS Fallon before the Lebanon Crisis. *Lawson*

Operation Prairie Fire and El Dorado Canyon

During the early months of 1986, the US Navy conducted Freedom of Navigation operations (FON) in the Gulf of Sidra, on the Libyan side of Muammar al-Gaddafi's so-called Line of Death. On March 24, Libyan SA-5 SAM sites launched several missiles at F-14 Tomcats orbiting off the coast near Sirte. Radar jamming and Navy HARM launches followed, resulting in further escalation by Libyan forces with the deployment of *Waheed,* a 250-ton French-built La Combattante II missile-equipped patrol boat. Considered a hostile threat, *Waheed* was engaged by Harpoon equipped VA-34 Intruders, leaving it dead in the water. Intruders from VA-85 finished the craft off with Mk. 20 Rockeye II CBUs.

The Libyan navy then dispatched a 560-ton Nanuchka II corvette that was engaged by Rockeye- and Harpoon-equipped Intruders assigned to VA-85, severely damaging the Libyan corvette. On the morning of March 25, the Libyan navy deployed a Nanuchka II corvette, *Ain Zaquit*. A-6Es assigned to VA-55 from USS *Coral Sea* engaged it with Mk. 20 Rockeye II CBU. VA-85 completed the task by sinking it with an AGM-84 Harpoon.

The *Ain Zaquit*, a 560-ton Soviet-built Nanuchka II Corvette, was disabled by Rockeye CBUs delivered by VA-55 A-6Es and sunk by a Harpoon launched by a VA-85 Intruder. *USN*

A-6E 158042 VA-85 displaying Operation Prairie Fire mission markings. *Author*

A-6E 161681 VA-55 displaying Operation Prairie Fire and El Dorado mission markings. *Author*

On April 5, 1986, proxies of Muammar al-Gaddafi bombed the La Belle disco, a popular night club in West Berlin. This terror attack resulted in the deaths of two Americans: Army sergeant James E. Goins, twenty-five, and Army sergeant Kenneth T. Ford, twenty-one. The event set the stage for Operation El Dorado Canyon, which began at 0200 hours local time on April 15. USS *America* and USS *Coral Sea* launched twenty-four Intruders consisting of A-6Es and KA-6Ds. The "Blue Blasters" of VA-34 were tasked with destroying the al-Jamahiriya military barracks in Benghazi. The "Warhorses" of VA-55 attacked Benina airfield on the outskirts of Benghazi. The attack lasted only twelve minutes and saw the destruction of several Libyan transport aircraft, two helicopters, and four MiG-23 fighters and the death of forty-five soldiers. Other participants included F/A-18A Hornets, E-2C Hawkeyes, EA-6B Prowlers, A-7E Corsair IIs, and EA-3B Skywarriors, as well as USAF F-111Fs and EF-111As, with aerial-refueling support provided by KC-10As and KC-135As.

A-6E 161679 VA-34 1986. *Sagnor*

A-6E 159317, assigned to VA-55, on the NAS Oceana ramp September 1986, displaying mission markings. *Author*

Aviation ordnancemen aboard the aircraft carrier USS *Coral Sea* prepare to load Mk. 82 Snakeye 500-pound bombs on a VA-55 A-6E Intruder aircraft before an airstrike on targets in Libya. *USN*

Blue Blaster KA-6D 151789 preparing to launch from USS *America*, 1986 cruise. *Sagnor*

Operation Praying Mantis

As part of a much-larger operation known as Earnest Will, Operation Praying Mantis was a retaliatory strike conducted on April 18, 1988, in response to USS *Samuel B. Roberts* (FFG-58) striking an Iranian mine during tanker escort duties in the Persian Gulf on April 14. At dawn on the eighteenth, VA-95 Intruders launched from USS *Enterprise* in support of the seizure of Iranian oil platforms used to attack allied shipping in the gulf. The A-6Es of VA-95 were armed with a variety of ordnance, including Laser-Guided Bombs (LGB), Harpoons, AGM-123 Skipper II, and Rockeye II CBUs. The Iranians responded with a gunboat that was quickly sunk by Navy surface ships. Additional threats emerged in the form of four high-speed gunboats. VA-95 targeted the lead boat with CBUs, and the remaining boats returned to port. Later that day it was learned other Iranian combatants were getting underway from Bandar Abbas, Iran. Intruders of VA-95 sent to investigate were fired upon by the Iranian Saam-class frigate *Sahand*. A-6E BuNo 156995 responded with one LGB, causing severe hull damage. The Intruder crew then followed up with a Harpoon, which struck *Sahand* amidships. Two Skipper II missiles were launched for good measure. One missed and the other impacted near the bridge. Another Iranian frigate, *Sabalan*, left port and was soon the target of another VA-95 Intruder, which struck it amidships with a 500-pound LGB, leaving it dead in the water. At this point the Pentagon called off Operation Praying Mantis, sparing *Sabalan* from total destruction.

April 18, 1988, A-6E 156995, assigned to VA-95, prepares to launch armed with an AGM-123 Skipper II, Mk. 20 Rockeye IIs, and AGM-84 Harpoon. *USN*

The Iranian frigate *Sahand* burning from bow to stern, April 18, 1988. *USN*

Operation Desert Shield and Desert Storm

The army of Iraq invaded Kuwait on August 2, 1990, overrunning the tiny nation within twenty-four hours. USS *Independence*, with VA-196 embarked, entered the Persian Gulf on August 8. The day before, USS *Dwight D. Eisenhower*, with VA-34 aboard, transited the Suez Canal from the Mediterranean Sea and took up a position in the Red Sea. This phase of the conflict was known as Operation Desert Shield. Coalition forces successfully countered a threatened invasion of Saudi Arabia and played a role in the economic blockade of Iraq.

VA-34 KA-6D 155691 manned up in preparation for a training mission, USS *Dwight D. Eisenhower*, March 1990. *Author's collection*

A-6E 158042 on the Intruder Country ramp, NAS Oceana, post–Desert Shield, April 17, 1991. During VA-34's 1990 cruise, the "Blue Blasters" integrated Night Vision Goggles (NVG) and the AGM-84E SLAM to the Intruder's already impressive arsenal. *Author*

A-6E 152905 VA-196 photographed on February 7, 1991, post–Desert Shield. While embarked aboard *Independence*, the Main Battery flew sorties from the Persian Gulf and the northern Arabian Sea. *Lawson*

RED SEA BATTLE GROUP BATTLE FORCE YANKEE

USS *Saratoga* (CV-60) VA-35

Saratoga transited the Suez Canal en route to the Red Sea on January 6 with VA-35 embarked. On January 17, 1991, A-6E 161668, assigned to VA-35, was shot down by a Roland surface-to-air missile during an attack against an airfield in western Iraq. Another Roland nearly claimed a second VA-35 Intruder the same night. The crew of 158539, Lt. John Snevely and Lt. Mark Eddy, had just commenced delivering high-drag Mk. 83s when the missile severely damaged their Intruder. They were forced to land at Al Jouf AB, Saudi Arabia. USS *Saratoga* departed the area on March 11, 1991. The Black Panthers returned to NAS Oceana, Virginia, on March 27, 1991.

A-6E 161668, assigned to VA-35, was downed by an Iraqi SAM on the first night of the war while attacking airfield H-3, in western Iraq. The crew, Lt. Robert Wetzel and Lt. Jeffrey Zaun, ejected; both were taken POW and released following forty-seven days in captivity. *Menth*

A-6E 158539 on the ground at Al Jouf, Saudi Arabia, following an emergency divert after being struck by an Iraqi SAM on January 17, 1991. Of interest is the AN/ALQ-167 "Bullwinkle" pod, used to jam Iraqi radars. *Ford*

USS *America* (CV-66) VA-85

America arrived on station in the Red Sea on January 15 with VA-85 embarked. The first strikes were launched from the Red Sea on the nineteenth. The "Black Falcons" initially struck oil storage facilities during daylight hours before moving on to other targets, including bridges and Scud launchers. *America* moved to the Persian Gulf on February 14, 1991, to join Battle Force ZULU, and VA-85 began preparing the battlefield for the Allied invasion of Iraq and Kuwait. VA-85 was tasked with the destruction of Silkworm cruise missile sites prior to the start of the ground war.

The crew of KA-6D 155598 gives a thumbs-up while returning to NAS Oceana from Operation Desert Storm, April 17, 1991. *Author*

Delivered as an A-6A on January 1, 1964, 149955 was modified to A-6B standards in 1970 and flew Iron Hand missions in Vietnam. Rebuilt as an A-6E in 1979 and then further modified with TRAM, it participated in Operation Desert Storm. Note the rows of mission markings below the canopy rail. *Author*

A6E 155602 suffered damage from AAA on February 15, 1991. Although able to return to USS *America*, the crew was unable to steer or to stop due to damaged hydraulics. The crew, LCmdr. J. Williams and Lt. L. Fox, were forced to eject and were recovered by the SAR helicopter. After removal of the AN/ALQ-167 Bullwinkle pod, 155602 was pushed over the side to clear the deck for returning strike aircraft. *USN*

USS *John F. Kennedy* (CV-67) VA-75

On December 3, 1990, *Kennedy*, with VA-75 SWIP Intruders aboard, transited the Suez Canal and took up station in the Red Sea. On January 17, 1991, 0120 hours local time, *John F. Kennedy* launched two major strikes comprising eighty sorties. On January 19, VA-75 Intruders flew into the heart of Iraq, making the first AGM-84E SLAM combat launch. By the time hostilities ceased on February 28, 1991, CVW-3 had mounted a total of 114 combat missions across the forty-two days of Operation Desert Storm; within those, VA-75's A-6Es had flown 417 sorties lasting 1,882.1 flying hours, while their KA-6Ds flew eighty-two tanking sorties lasting 271.8 hours. All of VA-75's Intruders returned safely to Oceana on March 27.

Only two squadrons (VA-145 and VA-75) flew the SWIP Intruder in Desert Storm. This example, A-6E 162199, displays a very impressive scoreboard for their March 27, 1991, NAS Oceana Desert Storm homecoming. *Author*

A-6E 162196 VA-75 returning to NAS Oceana, March 27, 1991. *Author*

PERSIAN GULF BATTLE GROUP BATTLE FORCE ZULU

USS *Ranger* (CV-61) VA-145 and VA-155

Ranger arrived in the north Persian Gulf on January 12 with VA-145 and VA-155 embarked. Both squadrons were assigned mostly night missions during Desert Storm. VA-145 and VA-155 flew their first combat sorties on January 17, 1991. Each Intruder was armed with twelve Mk. 36 DST mines—500-pound bombs with a fuze allowing it to function in shallow water. VA-155 did the mining, with VA-145, while attacking coastal defenses, becoming the first Intruder unit to deliver a HARM in combat. VA-145 flew 621 sorties against targets in Kuwait and Iraq, striking land- and sea-based targets. They were credited with destroying forty-eight artillery pieces, forty-one naval vessels, three chemical weapons storage facilities, and one bridge. VA-155 Intruders led *Ranger*'s last airstrike of Desert Storm. During the conflict they flew 635 sorties and delivered 2,289,940 pounds of ordnance. A-6E 152928, assigned to VA-155, was laying Mk. 36 mines near Umm Qasr Naval Base when AAA downed it on January 18, 1991. Lt. William Thompson and Lt. Charlie Turner were both KIA.

A-6E 162182 VA-145. *Grove*

A-6E 162182 displaying an impressive tally, including radar sites and ships destroyed. *Grove*

A-6E 152916 VA-155, January 1992. *Grove*

A-6E 152916 displays an impressive tally of targets destroyed by the squadron. The Texaco Star denotes 124 aerial refueling missions. *Grove*

USS *Midway* (CV-41), VA-115 and VA-185

Midway entered the Persian Gulf on December 21 with VA-115 and VA-185 embarked. Both Intruder squadrons took part in the first strikes of the war. Armed with six Mk. 83 1,000-pound bombs each, they hit Ahmed Al Jaber AB, Kuwait, and Shaibah airfield near Basra, Iraq. They next turned their attention to Iraqi naval vessels to prevent them from fleeing to Iran. Loadouts for these missions consisted of Rockeye II CBUs, LGBs, or Skippers IIs.

VA-115 Desert Storm mission markings. *Anselmo*

A-6E 157025 VA-115, August 26, 1991. *Anselmo*

A-6E 159575 VA-185 armed with a pair of Mk. 20 Rockeye IIs, LGB, and AN/ALQ-167. *Prince*

A-6E 155685 VA-185 Desert Storm on April 15, 1991. Of interest are the mission markings aft of the canopy. *Author's collection*

USS *Theodore Roosevelt* (CVN-71), VA-36 and VA-65
On January 19, USS *Theodore Roosevelt* entered the Persian Gulf with two A-6E Intruder squadrons (VA-36 and VA-65). On February 2, 1991, while attacking Iraqi navy vessels near Failaka Island, a VA-36 A-6E 155632 was brought down by an SA-7 SAM. The crew, LCmdr. Barry T. Cooke and Lt. Patrick Kelly Connor, went MIA and were later confirmed KIA.

VA-65 Intruders led strikes deep into Iraq before turning their attention to the Kuwait theater of operations, destroying tanks and artillery positions and prepping the battlefield for the invasion of Iraq and the liberation of Kuwait. VA-65 was also credited with sinking twenty-two Iraqi naval vessels. During one such day mission near Failaka Island, A-6E 155620 was hit by a large-caliber antiaircraft round. Although it did not detonate, it did punch a large hole in the wing. The crew, Lt. Jeff Martin and LCmdr. Don Quinn, diverted to Shaikh Isa, Bahrain. The Intruder was repaired and returned to fleet service. VA-65 also supported Operation Provide Comfort, the humanitarian efforts to relieve Iraqi pressure on the Kurds. USS *Theodore Roosevelt* returned to Norfolk on June 28. The air wing, CVW-8, conducted its fly-off on June 26.

During an early February mission to attack Iraqi boat traffic near Falafel Island, A-6E 155620 was hit by AAA, leaving a sizable hole in the starboard wing. The crew diverted to Shaikh Isa AB, Bahrain, landing without incident. *USN*

CVW-8 started Desert Storm with two Intruders painted in temporary desert camouflage. VA-65's 503 and VA-36's 533 retained these colors through mid-February. It was removed due to being less effective at medium altitudes than tactical paint scheme grays. 503 is shown with twelve Mk. 82 bombs. *Morgan*

VA-65's CAG bird, 161675, displays nose art applied after the war; in this case the cartoon cat wielding "The Big Stick" is referencing the ship's namesake, Theodore Roosevelt. The aircraft also has flak curtains installed in the cockpit. *Morgan*

A-6E 161675 VA-65 June 26, 1991, NAS Oceana homecoming. *Author*

As part of the postwar nose art contest held by CVW-8, VA-36 painted 155600 as "Heartless," using the squadron's radio call sign. *Morgan*

A-6E 155600 VA-36, June 26, 1991, NAS Oceana homecoming. *Author*

Sheikh Isa Air Base, Bahrain

The Bengals of Marine Squadron VMA(AW)-224 deployed to Sheikh Isa with ten TRAM equipped Intruders December 20, 1990, joining the Hawks of VMA(AW)-533, which arrived from Iwakuni, Japan, on August 24, 1990. Each squadron was assigned to fly night sorties tasked with destroying bridges, vehicle traffic, and other "hot targets" by using the Intruder's AMTI and TRAM FLIR to engage moving targets. The final combat sorties were flown on February 26, 1991, attacking the Iraqi army as they fled Kuwait on the "Highway of Death." Ordnance loadouts consisted of two GBU-10E/B 2,000-pound LGBs, twelve to twenty-four Mk. 82 500-pound and six Mk. 83 1,000-pound low-drag bombs, eleven Mk. 20 CBUs, or eight Mk-77 napalm bombs. VMA(AW)-224 departed Bahrain on March 26, 1991. Neither Marine unit lost an Intruder during Desert Shield and Desert Storm.

A-6E 157017 VMA(AW)-224. *Author*

A-6E VMA(AW)-533 Desert Storm, 1991. *USMC*

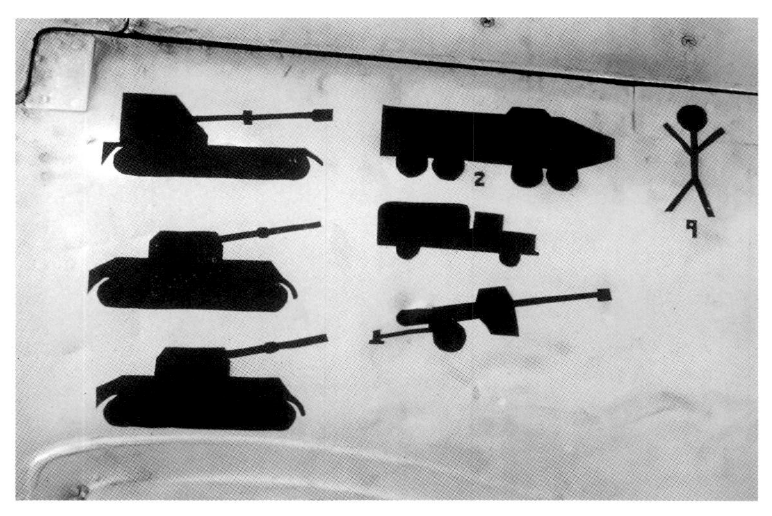

Crude but effective mission markings applied to A-6E 157017. *Author*

The Hawks applied a small bomb to represent each combat mission flown. This A-6E, 161663, appropriately named "Work Horse," displays an impressive tally of forty-five bombing missions flown during Desert Storm. *Author*

A-6E 161663, April 1, 1991. *Author*

Following Desert Storm, armed A-6Es patrolled Iraq's no-fly zone during Operations Northern Watch and Southern Watch. The Intruder's last bombs were delivered in anger on January 19, 1993, when VA-52 struck Iraqi AAA sites in retaliation for being fired upon. Note the pair of bomb silhouettes applied to A-6E 164379 while photographed on June 18, 1993. *Wilson*

CHAPTER 10
Sunset

The last Intruder, 164385, assigned to VA-145. It was written off when it ditched in the Persian Gulf on September 8, 1993. *Trombecky*

The Intruder was scheduled to be replaced by the McDonnell Douglas A-12 Avenger II. Unfortunately that program was canceled on January 7, 1991. The much-improved A-6F Intruder II was in development and would have filled the void left by the cancellation of the A-12. However, by the time the first A-6F flew (August 22, 1988), that program was also canceled, leaving no apparent successor for the A-6. Grumman continued to manufacture Intruders and the final A-6E (SWIP) Intruder, 164385, was delivered to VA-145 on April 1, 1992.

Meanwhile, at Grumman's St. Augustine, Florida, facility, A-6E Intruders were lined up waiting for the Systems Weapons Improvement Program improvements and new-built composite wings. These would have greatly extended the Intruder's life. The cancellation of the SWIP program followed the cancellation of the A-6F, and all A-6E modifications ceased. In a span of twenty-four hours these airframes went from being upgraded to scrap. Now what to do with more than sixty Intruders awaiting modifications? A Florida resident and Grumman employee, Steve Blalock, stepped in and proposed using the remaining Intruders to build an artificial reef off the Florida coast near St. Augustine. Grumman officials agreed, and following the removal of all hazardous materials, more than sixty Intruders were deposited at two locations in the Atlantic Ocean, an area now known as Intruder Reef and Intruder Alley.

Intruder squadrons began shutting down before A-6E modification and A-6F programs were canceled. On January 1, 1991, VA-55 was disestablished, followed by VA-185 on August 30, 1991. The pace quickened, with additional Navy and Marine squadrons being disestablished or transitioned to the F/A-18 Hornet. This author was present at MCAS Cherry Point on April 2, 1993, to witness the final flight of a Marine Intruder, A-6E 161681, assigned to VMA(AW)-332. The US Navy's first two Intruder squadrons, VA-75 and VA-196, would become the last. Each squadron participated in one final cruise: VA-196 aboard USS *Carl Vinson* (CVN-70) from May 14, 1996, to November 11, 1996, and VA-75 aboard USS *Enterprise* from June 28, 1996, to December 20, 1996. The last Intruder loss took place on June 4, 1996. A-6E 155704/NF-500 was towing a target banner during exercise "RIMPAC 96" when it became a target for the Phalanx antiaircraft defense system aboard the Japanese Self Defense Force destroyer JDS *Yugiri* (DD-153). The 20 mm Phalanx performed as advertised, inflicting mortal damage. The A-6E crew, Lt Cdr William E. Royster and Lt. Keith A. Douglas, ejected and were rescued. The final A-6 carrier launches took place on March 26, 1997, for VA-196 from USS *Carl Vinson*, and on March 12, 1997, for VA-75 from USS *Enterprise*. The Main Battery, VA-196, was officially disestablished on February 28, 1997. The "Sunday Punchers" of VA-75 officially disestablished on March 31, 1997. The last airworthy Intruder, BuNo 157027, assigned to VA-75, departed NAS Oceana on March 7, 1997. At the disestablishment ceremony on February 28, 1997, Secretary of the Navy John H. Dalton had this to say: "The A-6 exceeded our expectations anywhere, anytime." He further referred to the Intruder as "distinctive looking, and some would say, optically challenged." In conclusion, he repeated the refrain "Fighter pilots make movies but attack pilots make history."

A-6E 161681 VMA(AW)-332, April 2, 1993, MCAS Cherry Point, North Carolina. *Author*

Following the cancellation of the SWIP program, Grumman and the Navy were faced with the prospect of disposing of more than sixty Intruder hulks. Stripped of reusable parts and hazardous materials, they were used to create two artificial reefs off the coast of Florida. *Hildebrandt*

A-6E 157027 displaying a retro scheme on March 7, 1997, NAS Oceana. *Linn*

A-6E 159314, formerly assigned to VA-165, resting at AMARC, August 23, 1996. “Puff the Magic Dragon” nose art was applied by A03 Daniel Summers and AMH2 Kevin Welch. *Schuitemaker*

Vietnam and Persian Gulf veteran 149944 cocooned at AMARG, March 11, 2015. *Boschert*